PHOENIX FEATHERS

PHOENIX FEATHERS

A Collection of Mythical Monsters

Edited by Barbara Silverberg

ILLUSTRATED WITH OLD PRINTS

E. P. DUTTON & CO., INC. NEW YORK

3BUH000005928%

LIBRARY OF CONGRESS CATALOGING IN PUBLICATION DATA

Silverberg, Barbara, comp.   Phoenix feathers.

SUMMARY: A collection of legends and stories
about the exploits and magical powers of seven
mythical animals: the griffin, kraken, dragon,
unicorn, roc, basilisk, and phoenix.

1. Animals, Mythical—Stories. [1. Animals,
Mythical—Stories] I. Title.
PZ5.S595Ph   [Fic]   73–77459
ISBN 0–525–36985–6

Published simultaneously in Canada by Clarke,
Irwin & Company Limited, Toronto and Vancouver

Designed by Riki Levinson
Printed in the U.S.A.
First Edition

ACKNOWLEDGMENTS

For Bob and Carol and Terry,
whose love was my inspiration

CONTENTS

INTRODUCTION

We live in an age in which we tend not to believe in any creature we have not actually seen, whether behind bars in a zoo or stuffed in a museum. But until quite recently man had no reason for denying the existence of animals that we now know are imaginary. The world was so large that nobody could have seen it all. The whole of nature was so strange and unfathomable that none but God could comprehend its plan. Why, then, should man have questioned the existence of a strange beast he had not seen? The incredible, the miraculous, the unreasonable were accepted as a part of everyday life.

What caused man to believe in the existence of these particular creatures in the first place? One possibility is that certain mythical monsters were based on creatures that once existed and now are extinct. We know that some animals, such as the auk and the dodo, have become extinct in quite recent times, as a result of changes of climate or ecological balance, or even the predatory habits of man. Further back in history were the pterodactyl, the iguanadon, the brontosaur, all the fauna of the dinosaur age, creatures as strange as any the mind of man could invent. Could not one of these have survived into the age of man, and perhaps have developed into the image of a scaly dragon, as man's memory of the actual creature, now extinct, faded? Then, much later, as fossil bones of these gigantic reptiles were unearthed—bones from animals man had never seen, bones so great in size they must have belonged to some terrifying monster—belief in the existence of these mythical animals was reinforced.

Wishful thinking must have played a part in the creation of some of the mythical beasts. Man was constantly seeking some secret that would make him immortal, or invisible, or secure against injury or illness. Animals were believed to possess these secrets, the rarer the animal the stronger his magical powers. So man invented many strange creatures to protect him—the griffin, whose claw could detect poison, the unicorn, whose horn could save a dying man's life.

Animals were much used to symbolize natural phenomena in those early days, and this certainly is a clue to the origin of some of the mythical creatures. There can be no doubt that the phoenix represents the sun, rising from the ashes of its former self in golden glory. Similarly, other mysteries of nature were explained in terms of birds and animals, and then the creatures so described took on a life of their own and lingered on when their original significance was forgotten. Thus the wind was personified as a swift-flying horse, giving birth to the hippogriff legend; and, likewise, rain was worshiped in the form of the water-carrying dragon of China.

As man, in his search for religious truth, turned to deities in human and superhuman form, the animals he had once worshiped as gods were degraded into creatures of myth and fable. Animals became the form in which the anthropomorphic gods descended to earth, the disguise that Vishnu or Jupiter adopted when making appearances among men; when they needed to travel swiftly from one heavenly realm to another, the gods might take on the form of fabulous birds. All the Egyptian gods had their animal aspects—Horus wore the head of a hawk, Anubis that of a jackal; Osiris sometimes wore the head of a ram on a human body, and sometimes retained his human head and took on the body of a ram. Even the dead, according to Egyptian mythology, were thought to assume animal shape—a human-headed bird was a favorite representation of the soul of a man free of his earthbound body.

The enchanted world in which man once lived is lost to us now; much of what was once incomprehensible today seems obvious. Gone is the magic, gone is the terror, gone the jealous goddess who could turn her rival into a bear, gone the basilisk, a single glance at which caused certain death. With the advent of Christianity the attitude toward animals became more practical and more rational, and the pagan gods and their animal incarnations receded. The medieval Christian writers believed that every animal was created by God for the benefit of man—as a beast of burden, as food, or as the source of a remedy for some affliction. Many animal morality tales were conceived to illustrate these beliefs, and these nature stories were frequently collected in books called bestiaries, the earliest one dating from the first century A.D. The bestiaries were intended as serious statements of fact, but they included a few obviously imaginary creatures along with the many known and observable ones. The natural historians who compiled these and other "scientific" works of the Middle Ages were hampered by the lack of any real means of observation, and there seemed to be no desire on the part of either writer or reader to verify the scientific accuracy of the fantastic stories these books contained. People embraced legend and fable with great avidity, preferring them, it seems, to factual description.

These early historians obtained much of their information from hunters and fishermen, and from soldiers and sailors who had traveled to the far corners of the world. Such informants were prone to exaggerate what they had seen to impress their credulous listeners. In the years that followed, interest in travel for its own sake expanded, and direct observation of nature became a recognized scientific technique. Still, the reports of legendary lands and fabulous monsters continued to find their way into books—some the excusable misunderstandings and faulty observations of early naturalists who were trying to tell the truth, others folk beliefs that had persisted unchanged for many centuries. We can now turn to these picturesque histories for entertainment—Mandeville's *Travels* (1366), Gesner's *Historia Animalium* (1551), and Topsell's *History of Four-Footed Beasts* (1607) are good examples—and come away with detailed descriptions, complete even to illustrations, of such fabulous creatures as the unicorn, with its medicinal horn, the roc, which can carry off elephants, and the dragon, breathing flames.

So the mythical monsters come forth for us to examine —catalogued, illustrated, minutely described. Time alters their features, their forms shift and change, a nonsensical creature emerges from what was originally a credible animal. But the world may still hold surprises. Now, as we read the accounts of early historians, as we are amused by their simple acceptance of these fabulous beasts and entertained by the parade of fantasies that follows, let us remember that even *we* have not seen *all* the world. There are still unexplored jungles in Africa and South America, still vast oceans whose depths remain unknown, still untouched wildernesses in Central Australia—and unexpected beasts may yet come to life, unfamiliar animals, perhaps more bizarre than those included here, may some day be glimpsed. We would be wise not to make too strong a distinction between what is and what is not, what may have been and what will be.

Barbara Silverberg

NEW YORK, APRIL 1972

. . . He is tossed in a phantasmagoric bestiary, hurled past hooves and horns and gaping jaws. Here is the fount of invention. Here is the spring of life. How does one tell the dream from the undream? What are these chimeras, sphinxes, gorgons, basilisks, gryphons, krakens, hippogriffs, bandersnatches, jabberwocks, orcs, this whole horde of desperate marvels? Of time past? Of time yet unarrived? The turbulent dreams, nothing more, of the Fountain of Life?

—Robert Silverberg, *Son of Man*

I · THE GRIFFIN

Half bird, half beast, the griffin (or gryphon) was a mythical creature combining the features of the eagle and the lion, the king of birds and the king of beasts. Its head, wings, and forelegs were those of an eagle, its hindquarters and tail were those of a lion, its temperament was a mixture of fierceness and cunning. But its eagle-head was embellished by a pair of upright, pointed ears such as no bird ever wore. The claws of griffins were highly prized as an effective medicine against almost any disease, and it was said that the only way to acquire one was for a holy man to cure a griffin of some hurt or sickness and then to demand a claw as payment.

The griffin is one of the earliest of mythical monsters; a small golden statue of the beast, more than three thousand years old, was found in the royal tombs of Crete. Because of their reputation for fierceness, the griffins of early days were said to be in charge of guarding the gold mines of the gods against the greed of humans, as we are told by the first-century historian Pliny.

1

Pliny

THE ARIMASPI AND
THE GRIFFINS

In the vicinity also of those who dwell in the northern regions, and not far from the spot from which the north wind arises, and the place which is called its cave, and is known by the name of Geskleithron, the Arimaspi are said to exist, . . . a nation remarkable for having but one eye, and that placed in the middle of the forehead. This race is said to carry on a perpetual warfare with the griffins, a kind of monster, with wings, as they are commonly represented, for the gold which they dig out of the mines, and which these wild beasts retain and keep watch over with a singular degree of cupidity, while the Arimaspi are equally desirous to get possession of it.

> Sir John Mandeville, an English traveler of the fourteenth century, claimed to have seen these mythical creatures in their native land. Mandeville's book of travels was widely read and accepted in medieval Europe; he was a fine storyteller, though perhaps not an entirely reliable authority. Here we have his description of the griffin.

Sir John Mandeville

GRIFFINS IN THE LAND
OF BACHARY

From this land men shall go to the land of Bachary, where are many wicked men and fell. In this land are trees that bear wool, as it were of sheep, of which they make cloth.

In this land also are many ypotams, that dwell some time upon land and some time on the water; and they are half man and half horse. And they eat men whereso they may get them, no meat gladlier. And in that land are many griffins, more than in any other country else. And some men say that they have the shape of an eagle before, and behind the shape of a lion; and sickerly they say sooth. Nevertheless the griffin is more and stronger than eight lions of these countries, and greater and stalworther than a hundred eagles. For certainly he will bear til his nest flying a great horse and a man upon him, or two oxen yoked together, as they go sammen [together] at the plough. For he has nails upon his feet als great and als long as they were oxen horns, but they are wonder sharp. And of those nails men make cups for to drink of, as we do of the horns of bugles [bulls]; and of the backs of his feathers they make strong bows for to shoot with. . . .

The griffin is one of the most popular beasts in heraldry, appearing on numerous coats of arms, including that of the City of London. Over the years he has lost much of his reputation for ferocity, so that in modern stories he is often described in almost affectionate terms. Frank R. Stockton, a popular writer of fairy tales and children's stories in the late nineteenth century, and for a time an editor of *St. Nicholas Magazine,* published just for children, tells a marvelous tale of a griffin who discovers a statue of himself.

Frank R. Stockton

THE GRIFFIN AND THE
MINOR CANON

Over the great door of an old, old church, which stood in a quiet town of a faraway land, there was carved in stone the figure of a large griffin. The old-time sculptor had done his work with great care, but the image he had made was not a pleasant one to look at. It had a large head with enormous open mouth and savage teeth; from its back arose great wings, armed with sharp hooks and prongs; it had stout legs in front with projecting claws; but there were no legs behind—the body running out into a long and powerful tail, finished off at the end with a barbed point. This tail was coiled up under him, the end sticking up just back of his wings.

The sculptor, or the people who had ordered this stone figure, had evidently been very much pleased with it, for little copies of it, also in stone, had been placed here and there along the sides of the church, not very far from the ground, so that people could easily look at them and ponder on their curious form. There were a great many other sculptures on the outside of this church —saints, martyrs, grotesque heads of men, beasts, and birds, as well as those of other creatures which cannot be named because nobody knows exactly what they were— but none were so curious and interesting as the great griffin over the door and the little griffins on the sides of the church.

A long, long distance from the town, in the midst of dreadful wilds scarcely known to man, there dwelt the Griffin whose image had been put up over the church door. In some way or other, the old-time sculptor had

4

seen him and afterward, to the best of his memory, had copied his figure in stone. The Griffin had never known this, until, hundreds of years afterward, he heard from a bird, from a wild animal, or in some manner, which it is not now easy to find out, that there was a likeness of him on the old church in the distant town. Now, this Griffin had no idea how he looked. He had never seen a mirror, and the streams where he lived were so turbulent and violent that a quiet piece of water, which would reflect the image of anything looking into it, could not be found. Being, as far as could be ascertained, the very last of his race, he had never seen another griffin. Therefore it was, that, when he heard of this stone image of himself, he became very anxious to know what he looked like, and at last he determined to go to the old church and see for himself what manner of being he was. So he started off from the dreadful wilds and flew on and on until he came to the countries inhabited by men, where his appearance in the air created great consternation; but he alighted nowhere, keeping up a steady flight until he reached the suburbs of the town which had his image on its church. Here, late in the afternoon, he alighted in a green meadow by the side of a brook and stretched himself on the grass to rest. His great wings were tired, for he had not made such a long flight in a century or more.

The news of his coming spread quickly over the town, and the people, frightened nearly out of their wits by the arrival of so extraordinary a visitor, fled into their houses and shut themselves up. The Griffin called loudly for someone to come to him, but the more he called, the more afraid the people were to show themselves. At length he saw two laborers hurrying to their homes through the fields, and in a terrible voice he commanded them to stop. Not daring to disobey, the men stood, trembling.

"What is the matter with you all?" cried the Griffin.

5

"Is there not a man in your town who is brave enough to speak to me?"

"I think," said one of the laborers, his voice shaking so that his words could hardly be understood, "that—perhaps—the Minor Canon—would come."

"Go call him, then!" said the Griffin. "I want to see him."

The Minor Canon, who filled a subordinate position in the old church, had just finished the afternoon services and was coming out of a side door with three aged women who had formed the weekday congregation. He was a young man of a kind disposition and very anxious to do good to the people of the town. Apart from his duties in the church, where he conducted services every weekday, he visited the sick and the poor, counseled and assisted persons who were in trouble, and taught a school composed entirely of the bad children in the town with whom nobody else would have anything to do. Whenever the people wanted something difficult done for them, they always went to the Minor Canon. Thus it was that the laborer thought of the young priest when he found that someone must come and speak to the Griffin.

The Minor Canon had not heard of the strange event, which was known to the whole town except himself and the three old women, and when he was informed of it and was told that the Griffin had asked to see him, he was greatly amazed and frightened.

"Me!" he exclaimed. "He has never heard of me! What should he want with *me*?"

"Oh, you must go instantly!" cried the two men. "He is very angry now because he has been kept waiting so long; and nobody knows what may happen if you don't hurry to him."

The poor Canon would rather have had his hand cut off than to go out to meet an angry griffin; but he felt that it was his duty to go, for it would be a woeful thing if injury should come to the people of the town because he was not brave enough to obey the summons of the Griffin. So, pale and frightened, he started off.

"Well," said the Griffin, as soon as the young man came near, "I am glad to see that there is someone who has the courage to come to me."

The Minor Canon did not feel very courageous, but he bowed his head.

"Is this the town," said the Griffin, "where there is a church with a likeness of myself over one of the doors?"

The Minor Canon looked at the frightful creature before him and saw that it was, without doubt, exactly like the stone image on the church. "Yes," he said. "You are right."

"Well, then," said the Griffin, "will you take me to it? I wish very much to see it."

The Minor Canon instantly thought that if the Griffin entered the town without the people knowing what he came for, some of them would probably be frightened to death, and so he sought to gain time to prepare their minds.

"It is growing dark now," he said, very much afraid, as he spoke, that his words might enrage the Griffin, "and objects on the front of the church cannot be seen clearly. It will be better to wait until morning if you wish to get a good view of the stone image of yourself."

"That will suit me very well," said the Griffin. "I see you are a man of good sense. I am tired, and I will take a nap here on this soft grass, while I cool my tail in the little stream that runs near me. The end of my tail gets red-hot when I am angry or excited, and it is quite warm now. So you may go, but be sure and come early tomorrow morning and show me the way to the church."

The Minor Canon was glad enough to take his leave

7

and hurried into the town. In front of the church he found a great many people assembled to hear his report of his interview with the Griffin. When they found that he had not come to spread ruin and devastation but simply to see his stony likeness on the church, they showed neither relief nor gratification but began to upbraid the Minor Canon for consenting to conduct the creature into the town.

"What could I do?" cried the young man. "If I should not bring him, he would come himself and perhaps end by setting fire to the town with his red-hot tail."

Still the people were not satisfied, and a great many plans were proposed to prevent the Griffin from coming into the town. Some elderly persons urged that the young men should go out and kill him; but the young men scoffed at such a ridiculous idea. Then someone said that it would be a good thing to destroy the stone image so that the Griffin would have no excuse for entering the town; and this proposal was received with such favor that many of the people ran for hammers, chisels, and crowbars with which to tear down and break up the stone griffin. But the Minor Canon resisted this plan with all the strength of his mind and body. He assured the people that this action would enrage the Griffin beyond measure, for it would be impossible to conceal from him that his image had been destroyed during the night. But the people were so determined to break up the stone griffin that the Minor Canon saw that there was nothing for him to do but to stay there and protect it. All night he walked up and down in front of the church door, keeping away the men who brought ladders, by which they might mount to the great stone griffin and knock it to pieces with their hammers and crowbars. After many hours the people were obliged to give up their attempts and went home to sleep; but the

Minor Canon remained at his post till early morning, and then he hurried away to the field where he had left the Griffin.

The monster had just awakened, and rising to his forelegs and shaking himself, he said that he was ready to go into the town. The Minor Canon, therefore, walked back, the Griffin flying slowly through the air, at a short distance above the head of his guide. Not a person was to be seen in the streets, and they proceeded directly to the front of the church, where the Minor Canon pointed out the stone griffin.

The real Griffin settled down in the little square before the church and gazed earnestly at his sculptured likeness. For a long time he looked at it. First he put his head on one side, and then he put it on the other; then he shut his right eye and gazed with his left, after which he shut his left eye and gazed with his right. Then he moved a little to one side and looked at the image, then he moved the other way.

After awhile, he said to the Minor Canon, who had been standing by all this time, "It is, it must be, an excellent likeness! That breadth between the eyes, that expansive forehead, those massive jaws! I feel that it must resemble me. If there is any fault to find with it, it is that the neck seems a little stiff. But that is nothing. It is an admirable likeness—admirable!"

The Griffin sat looking at his image all the morning and all the afternoon. The Minor Canon had been afraid to go away and leave him and had hoped all through the day that he would soon be satisfied with his inspection and fly away home. But by evening the poor young man was utterly exhausted and felt that he must eat and sleep. He frankly admitted this fact to the Griffin and asked him if he would not like something to eat. He said this because he felt obliged in politeness to do so, but as soon

9

as he had spoken the words, he was seized with dread lest the monster should demand half a dozen babies or some tempting repast of that kind.

"Oh, no," said the Griffin. "I never eat between the equinoxes. At the vernal and at the autumnal equinox I take a good meal, and that lasts me for half a year. I am extremely regular in my habits and do not think it healthful to eat at odd times. But if you need food, go and get it, and I will return to the soft grass where I slept last night and take another nap."

The next day the Griffin came again to the little square before the church, and remained there until evening, steadfastly regarding the stone griffin over the door. The Minor Canon came once or twice to look at him, and the Griffin seemed very glad to see him; but the young clergyman could not stay as he had done before, for he had many duties to perform. Nobody went to the church, but the people came to the Minor Canon's house and anxiously asked him how long the Griffin was going to stay.

"I do not know," he answered, "but I think he will soon be satisfied with regarding his stone likeness, and then he will go away."

But the Griffin did not go away. Morning after morning he came to the church, but after a time he did not stay there all day. He seemed to have taken a great fancy to the Minor Canon and followed him about as he pursued his various avocations. He would wait for him at the side door of the church, for the Minor Canon held services every day, morning and evening, though nobody came now. "If anyone should come," he said to himself, "I must be found at my post." When the young man came out, the Griffin would accompany him in his visits to the sick and the poor and would often look into the windows of the schoolhouse where the Minor Canon was teaching his unruly scholars. All the other schools were closed, but the parents of the Minor Canon's scholars forced them to go to school, because they were so bad they could not endure them all day at home—griffin or no griffin. But it must be said they generally behaved very well when that great monster sat up on his tail and looked in at the schoolroom window.

When it was perceived that the Griffin showed no sign of going away, all the people who were able to do so left the town. The canons and the higher officers of the church had fled away during the first day of the Griffin's visit, leaving behind only the Minor Canon and some of the men who opened the doors and swept the church. All the citizens who could afford it shut up their houses and traveled to distant parts, and only the working people and the poor were left behind. After some days, these ventured to go about and attend to their business, for if they did not work they would starve. They were getting a little used to seeing the Griffin, and having been told that he did not eat between equinoxes, they did not feel so much afraid of him as before.

Day by day the Griffin became more and more attached to the Minor Canon. He kept near him a great part of the time and often spent the night in front of the little house where the young clergyman lived alone. This strange companionship was often burdensome to the Minor Canon; but on the other hand, he could not deny that he derived a great deal of benefit and instruction from it. The Griffin had lived for hundreds of years and had seen much, and he told the Minor Canon many wonderful things.

"It is like reading an old book," said the young clergyman to himself; "but how many books I would have had to read before I would have found out what the Griffin has told me about the earth, the air, the water, about minerals and metals and growing things and all the wonders of the world!''

Thus the summer went on and drew toward its close. And now the people of the town began to be very much troubled again.

"It will not be long," they said, "before the autumnal equinox is here, and then that monster will want to eat. He will be dreadfully hungry, for he has taken so much exercise since his last meal. He will devour our children. Without doubt, he will eat them all. What is to be done?"

To this question no one could give an answer, but all agreed that the Griffin must not be allowed to remain until the approaching equinox. After talking over the matter a great deal, a crowd of the people went to the Minor Canon, at a time when the Griffin was not with him.

"It is all your fault," they said, "that that monster is among us. You brought him here, and you ought to see that he goes away. It is only on your account that he stays here at all, for although he visits his image every day, he is with you the greater part of the time. If you were not here, he would not stay. It is your duty to go away, and then he will follow you, and we shall be free from the dreadful danger which hangs over us."

"Go away!" cried the Minor Canon, greatly grieved at being spoken to in such a way. "Where shall I go? If I go to some other town, shall I not take this trouble there? Have I a right to do that?"

"No," said the people, "you must not go to any other town. There is no town far enough away. You must go to the dreadful wilds where the Griffin lives; and then he will follow you and stay there."

They did not say whether or not they expected the Minor Canon to stay there also, and he did not ask them anything about it. He bowed his head and went into his house to think. The more he thought, the more clear it became to his mind that it was his duty to go away and thus free the town from the presence of the Griffin.

That evening he packed a leathern bag full of bread and meat, and early the next morning he set out on his journey to the dreadful wilds. It was a long, weary, and doleful journey, especially after he had gone beyond the habitations of men, but the Minor Canon kept on bravely and never faltered. The way was longer than he had expected, and his provisions soon grew so scanty that he was obliged to eat but a little every day; but he kept up his courage and pressed on, and after many days of toilsome travel, he reached the dreadful wilds.

When the Griffin found that the Minor Canon had left the town, he seemed sorry but showed no disposition to go and look for him. After a few days had passed, he became much annoyed and asked some of the people where the Minor Canon had gone. But although the citizens had been so anxious that the young clergyman should go to the dreadful wilds, thinking that the Griffin would immediately follow him, they were now afraid to mention the Minor Canon's destination, for the monster seemed angry already, and if he should suspect their trick, he would doubtless become very much enraged. So everyone said he did not know, and the Griffin wandered about disconsolate. One morning he looked into the Minor Canon's schoolhouse, which was always empty now, and thought that it was a shame that everything should suffer on account of the young man's absence.

"It does not matter so much about the church," he said, "for nobody went there; but it is a pity about the school. I think I will teach it myself until he returns."

It was the hour for opening the school, and the Griffin went inside and pulled the rope which rang the school bell. Some of the children who heard the bell ran in to see what was the matter, supposing it to be a joke of one of their companions; but when they saw the Griffin, they stood astonished and scared.

"Go tell the other scholars," said the monster, "that school is about to open, and that if they are not all here in ten minutes, I shall come after them."

In seven minutes every scholar was in place.

Never was seen such an orderly school. Not a boy or girl moved or uttered a whisper. The Griffin climbed into the master's seat, his wide wings spread on each side of him, because he could not lean back in his chair while they stuck out behind, and his great tail coiled around in front of the desk, the barbed end sticking up, ready to tap any boy or girl who might misbehave. The Griffin now addressed the scholars, telling them that he intended to teach them while their master was away. In speaking he endeavored to imitate, as far as possible, the mild and gentle tones of the Minor Canon, but it must be admitted that in this he was not very successful. He had paid a good deal of attention to the studies of the school, and he determined not to attempt to teach them anything new but to review them in what they had been studying; so he called up the various classes and questioned them upon their previous lessons. The children racked their brains to remember what they had learned. They were so afraid of the Griffin's displeasure that they recited as they had never recited before. One of the boys, far down in his class, answered so well that the Griffin was astonished.

"I should think you would be at the head," said he. "I am sure you have never been in the habit of reciting so well. Why is this?"

"Because I did not choose to take the trouble," said the boy, trembling in his boots. He felt obliged to speak the truth, for all the children thought that the great eyes of the Griffin could see right through them and that he would know when they told a falsehood.

"You ought to be ashamed of yourself," said the Griffin. "Go down to the very tail of the class, and if you are not at the head in two days, I shall know the reason why."

The next afternoon this boy was number one.

It was astonishing how much these children now learned of what they had been studying. It was as if they had been educated over again. The Griffin used no severity toward them, but there was a look about him which made them unwilling to go to bed until they were sure they knew their lessons for the next day.

The Griffin now thought that he ought to visit the sick and the poor; and he began to go about the town for this purpose. The effect upon the sick was miraculous. All except those who were very ill indeed jumped from their beds when they heard he was coming and declared themselves quite well. To those who could not get up, he gave herbs and roots, which none of them had ever before thought of as medicines but which the Griffin had seen used in various parts of the world; and most of them recovered. But for all that, they afterward said that no matter what happened to them, they hoped that they should never again have such a doctor coming to their bedsides, feeling their pulses and looking at their tongues.

As for the poor, they seemed to have utterly disappeared. All those who had depended upon charity for their daily bread were now at work in some way or other, many of them offering to do odd jobs for their neighbors just for the sake of their meals—a thing which before had been seldom heard of in the town. The Griffin could find no one who needed his assistance.

The summer had now passed, and the autumnal equinox was rapidly approaching. The citizens were in a state

15

of great alarm and anxiety. The Griffin showed no signs of going away but seemed to have settled himself permanently among them. In a short time the day for his semiannual meal would arrive, and then what would happen? The monster would certainly be very hungry and would devour all their children.

Now they greatly regretted and lamented that they had sent away the Minor Canon; he was the only one on whom they could have depended in this trouble, for he could talk freely with the Griffin and so find out what could be done. But it would not do to be inactive. Some step must be taken immediately. A meeting of the citizens was called, and two old men were appointed to go and talk to the Griffin. They were instructed to offer to prepare a splendid dinner for him on equinox day—one which would entirely satisfy his hunger. They would offer him the fattest mutton, the most tender beef, fish, and game of various sorts, and anything of the kind that he might fancy. If none of these suited, they were to mention that there was an orphan asylum in the next town.

"Anything would be better," said the citizens, "than to have our dear children devoured."

The old men went to the Griffin, but their propositions were not received with favor.

"From what I have seen of the people of this town," said the monster, "I do not think I could relish anything which was prepared by them. They appear to be all cowards, and therefore mean and selfish. As for eating one of them, old or young, I could not think of it for a moment. In fact, there was only one creature in the whole place for whom I could have had any appetite and that is the Minor Canon, who has gone away. He was brave and good and honest, and I think I should have relished him."

16

"Ah!" said one of the old men very politely. "In that case I wish we had not sent him to the dreadful wilds!"

"What!" cried the Griffin. "What do you mean? Explain instantly what you are talking about!"

The old man, terribly frightened at what he had said, was obliged to tell how the Minor Canon had been sent away by the people, in the hope that the Griffin might be induced to follow him.

When the monster heard this, he became furiously angry. He dashed away from the old men, and spreading his wings, flew backward and forward over the town. He was so much excited that his tail became red-hot and glowed like a meteor against the evening sky. When at last he settled down in the little field where he usually rested and thrust his tail into the brook, the steam arose like a cloud, and the water of the stream ran hot through the town. The citizens were greatly frightened and bitterly blamed the old man for telling about the Minor Canon.

"It is plain," they said, "that the Griffin intended at last to go and look for him, and we should have been saved. Now who can tell what misery you have brought upon us."

The Griffin did not remain long in the little field. As soon as his tail was cool he flew to the town hall and rang the bell. The citizens knew that they were expected to come there, and although they were afraid to go, they were still more afraid to stay away; and they crowded into the hall. The Griffin was on the platform at one end, flapping his wings and walking up and down, and the end of his tail was still so warm that it slightly scorched the boards as he dragged it after him.

When everybody who was able to come was there, the Griffin stood still and addressed the meeting.

"I have had a contemptible opinion of you," he said,

17

"ever since I discovered what cowards you are, but I had no idea that you were so ungrateful, selfish, and cruel as I now find you to be. Here was your Minor Canon, who labored day and night for your good and thought of nothing else but how he might benefit you and make you happy; and as soon as you imagine yourselves threatened with a danger—for well I know you are dreadfully afraid of me—you send him off, caring not whether he returns or perishes, hoping thereby to save yourselves. Now, I had conceived a great liking for that young man and had intended, in a day or two, to go and look him up. But I have changed my mind about him. I shall go and find him, but I shall send him back here to live among you, and I intend that he shall enjoy the reward of his labor and his sacrifices. Go, some of you, to the officers of the church, who so cowardly ran away when I first came here, and tell them never to return to this town under penalty of death. And if, when your Minor Canon comes back to you, you do not bow yourselves before him, put him in the highest place among you, and serve and honor him all his life, beware of my terrible vengeance! There were only two good things in this town: the Minor Canon and the stone image of myself over your church door. One of these you have sent away, and the other I shall carry away myself."

With these words he dismissed the meeting, and it was time, for the end of his tail had become so hot that there was danger of its setting fire to the building.

The next morning the Griffin came to the church, and tearing the stone image of himself from its fastenings over the great door, he grasped it with his powerful fore-legs and flew up into the air. Then, after hovering over the town for a moment, he gave his tail an angry shake and took up his flight to the dreadful wilds. When he reached this desolate region, he set the stone griffin upon a ledge of a rock which rose in front of the dismal cave he called his home. There the image occupied a position somewhat similar to that it had had over the church door; and the Griffin, panting with the exertion of carrying such an enormous load to so great a distance, lay down upon the ground and regarded it with much satisfaction. When he felt somewhat rested, he went to look for the Minor Canon. He found the young man, weak and half starved, lying under the shadow of a rock. After picking him up and carrying him to his cave, the Griffin flew away to a distant marsh where he procured some roots and herbs which he well knew were strengthening and beneficial to man, although he had never tasted them himself. After eating these, the Minor Canon was greatly revived and sat up and listened while the Griffin told him what had happened in the town.

"Do you know," said the monster, when he had finished, "that I have had, and still have, a great liking for you?"

"I am very glad to hear it," said the Minor Canon, with his usual politeness.

"I am not at all sure that you would be," said the Griffin, "if you thoroughly understood the state of the case, but we will not consider that now. If some things were different, other things would be otherwise. I have been so enraged by discovering the manner in which you have been treated that I have determined that you shall at last enjoy the rewards and honors to which you are entitled. Lie down and have a good sleep, and then I will take you back to the town."

As he heard these words, a look of trouble came over the young man's face.

"You need not give yourself any anxiety," said the Griffin, "about my return to the town. I shall not remain there. Now that I have that admirable likeness of myself in front of my cave, where I can sit at my leisure and gaze upon its noble features and magnificent proportions, I have no wish to see that abode of cowardly and selfish people."

The Minor Canon, relieved from his fears, lay back and dropped into a doze; and when he was sound asleep, the Griffin took him up and carried him back to the town. He arrived just before daybreak, and putting the young man gently on the grass in the little field where he himself used to rest, the monster, without having been seen by any of the people, flew back to his home.

When the Minor Canon made his appearance in the morning among the citizens, the enthusiasm and cordiality with which he was received were truly wonderful. He was taken to a house which had been occupied by one of the banished high officers of the place, and everyone was anxious to do all that could be done for his health and comfort. The people crowded into the church when he held services, so that the three old women who used to be his weekday congregation could not get to the best seats, which they had always been in the habit of taking; and the parents of the bad children determined to reform them at home, in order that he might be spared the trouble of keeping up his former school. The Minor Canon was appointed to the highest office of the old church, and before he died, he became a bishop.

During the first years after his return from the dreadful wilds, the people of the town looked up to him as a man to whom they were bound to honor and reverence; but they often also looked up to the sky to see if there were any signs of the Griffin coming back. However, in the course of time, they learned to honor and reverence their former Minor Canon without the fear of being punished if they did not do so.

But they need never have been afraid of the Griffin.

The autumnal equinox day came around, and the monster ate nothing. If he could not have the Minor Canon, he did not care for anything. So, lying down, with his eyes fixed upon the great stone griffin, he gradually declined and died. It was a good thing for some of the people of the town that they did not know this.

If you should ever visit the old town, you would still see the little griffins on the sides of the church; but the great stone griffin that was over the door is gone.

II · THE KRAKEN

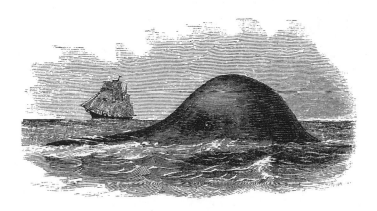

The kraken is a sea monster that appears in the mythology of Scandinavia. It is so large, the legends say, that when it rises to the surface to bask in the sun, it is often mistaken for an island by unwary sailors. And when it sinks back down to its lair again, it causes such a whirlpool that any ship in the vicinity is sucked down to destruction.

Despite its menace to navigation, fishermen are indirectly helped by the kraken, for when it rises from the ocean floor, large schools of fish are forced up with it. Men who take care not to linger too long can net a rich haul, but if they prove too greedy they may be stranded on the back of the rising monster.

The kraken most closely resembles a giant squid, a larger relative of the octopus. This creature is monstrous enough even without the embellishments of legend—giant squids have been known to reach lengths of more than eighty feet.

The first published reference to the kraken is found in Archbishop Olaus Magnus' *History of the Northern People,* dated 1555.

Archbishop Olaus Magnus

FROM THE POLYPUS ON THE COASTS OF NORWAY

On the Coasts of *Norway* there is a Polypus, or creature with many feet, which hath a pipe on his back, whereby he puts to Sea, and he moves that sometimes to the right, and sometimes to the left. Moreover, with his Legs as it were by hollow places, dispersed here and there, and by his Toothed Nippers, he fastneth on every living Creature that comes near to him, that wants blood. Whatever he eats he heaps up in the holes where he resides: Then he casts out the Skins, having eaten the flesh, and hunts after fishes that swim to them: Also he casts out the shels, and hard outsides of Crabs that remain. He changeth by the colour of the stone he sticks unto, especially when he is frighted at the sight of his Enemy, the Conger. He hath four great middle feet, in all eight; a little body, which the great feet make amends for. He hath also some small feet that are shadowed and can scarce be perceived. By these he sustains, moves, and defends himself, and takes hold of what is from him: and he lies on his back upon the stones, that he can scarce be gotten off, onlesse you put some stinking smell to him.

Legends of this monstrous sea creature proliferated in the centuries that followed: tales of sailors being snatched from the decks of their ships by the long, waving tentacles of the kraken, and of ships being dragged to the ocean floor by a kraken disturbed in the midst of a sunbath. In the eighteenth century the Norwegian naturalist Erich Pontoppidan, Bishop of Bergen, published a detailed description of the

24

kraken in *The Natural History of Norway* (1751).
This book is a combination of factual information
collected through careful observations and of fantastic fables and legends that Pontoppidan apparently believed to be true. His work makes delightful
reading, as the following selection reveals.

Bishop Erich Pontoppidan

THE LARGEST SEA-MONSTER IN THE WORLD

I am now come to the third and incontestably the largest
Sea-monster in the world; it is called Kraken, Kraxen,
or, as some name it, Krabben, that word being applied
by way of eminence to this creature. This last name seems
indeed best to agree with the description of this creature,
which is round, flat, and full of arms, or branches. . . .

Our fishermen unanimously affirm, and without the
least variation in their accounts, that when they row out
several miles to sea, particularly in the hot Summer days,
and by their situation (which they know by taking a
view of certain points of land) expect to find eighty or
a hundred fathoms water, it often happens that they do
not find above twenty or thirty, and sometimes less. At
these places they generally find the greatest plenty of
Fish, especially Cod and Ling. Their lines they say are
no sooner out than they may draw them up with the
hooks all full of Fish; by this they judge that the Kraken
is at the bottom. They say this creature causes those unnatural shallows mentioned above, and prevents their
sounding. These the fishermen are always glad to find,
looking upon them as a means of taking abundance of
Fish. There are sometimes twenty boats or more got

25

together, and throwing out their lines at a moderate
distance from each other; and the only thing they then
have to observe is, whether the depth continues the same,
which they know by their lines, or whether it grows
shallower by their seeming to have less water. If this last
be the case, they find that the Kraken is raising himself
nearer the surface, and then it is not time for them to
stay any longer; they immediately leave off fishing, take
to their oars, and get away as fast as they can. When they
have reached the usual depth of the place, and find themselves out of danger, they lie upon their oars, and in a
few minutes after they see this enormous monster come
up to the surface of the water; he there shows himself
sufficiently, though his whole body does not appear,
which in all likelihood no human eye ever beheld . . . .,
its back or upper part, which seems to be in appearance
about an English mile and an half in circumference
(some say more, but I chuse the least for greater cer-
tainty) , looks at first like a number of small islands, surrounded with something that floats and fluctuates like
sea-weeds. Here and there a larger rising is observed like
sand-banks, on which various kinds of small Fishes are
seen continually leaping about till they roll off into the
water from the sides of it; at last several bright points or
horns appear, which grow thicker and thicker the higher
they rise above the surface of the water, and sometimes
they stand up as high and large as the masts of middle-
siz'd vessels.

It seems these are the creature's arms, and, it is said,
if they were to lay hold of the largest man of war, they
would pull it down to the bottom. After this monster
has been on the surface of the water a short time, it
begins slowly to sink again, and then the danger is as
great as before; because the motion of his sinking causes

26

such a swell in the sea, and such an eddy or whirlpool, that it draws every thing down with it. . . .

The Kraken has never been known to do any great harm, except they have taken away the lives of those who consequently could not bring the tidings. I have never heard but one instance mentioned, which happened a few years ago near Fridrichstad, in the diocese of Agger-huus. They say that two fishermen accidentally, and to their great surprise, fell into such a spot on the water as has been before described, full of a thick slime, almost like a morass. They immediately strove to get out of this place, but they had not time to turn quick enough to save themselves from one of the Kraken's horns, which crushed the head of the boat, so that it was with great difficulty they saved their lives on the wreck, tho' the weather was as calm as possible; for these monsters, like the Sea-snake, never appear at other times.

And now, here is a modern version of the kraken legend, a tense and exciting sea adventure involving a submarine, a kraken, and some clever and not-so-clever sailors. This story, written by Frederick Engel-hardt in 1940, has become a classic in its own time.

Frederick Engelhardt

THE KRAKEN

Like a sounding whale plagued by hunters, the *U-213* lifted her fluked tail and plunged toward the bottom. Down, down she went, trailing a necklace of bubbles forced from her ballast tanks. Now a darker streamer was torn from her side by the rushing water and wafted to the surface. There it spread, glowing with myriad colors under the cold northern sun, to mark the descent of the steel leviathan.

In the bowels of the monster silence reigned, save for the intrusive rumbling of the waters as she clove through the depths. The pale lights made masks of the faces of the crew, who, braced in grotesque attitudes against the steep descent, waited in stolid patience for orders—or death. Amidships, in the cluttered control chamber, Korvettenkapitan Lothar Diedrich fixed his monocle in a dispassionate gaze on the crawling needles of the fathometer.

When the point quivered on "40" he barked an order and a square, bronzed giant beside him wrenched at the spokes of a wheel set into the steel bulkhead. The needle slowed in its course around the dial and the deck was level. The rumbling of the water died away to a faint murmur. Diedrich released his hold on the periscope standard and turned to his second in command.

"We fooled them," he remarked in a cold, brittle tone. "One would think they would get wise to that old oil trick. But the *Dummkopf* will steam back to Kirkwall at full speed to brag that another raider has been destroyed. Here"—he caught a headphone set from an impassive sailor and held it out—"listen. Their propeller beat grows fainter already."

Oberleutnant Graf Gunther von Rothberg accepted the phones and clapped one to his ear. The rhythmic throbbing of the English destroyer's screws was barely audible, even though amplified by the sensitive audiophone.

"This calls for a toast," he grinned at the bearded commander.

"It will have to be *Schnapps,* then," the other retorted.

"The champagne we took from that Frenchman two weeks ago is all gone. Call the steward."

While the crew looked on woodenly, but nonetheless thirstily, the two Junkers, with the assistance of the engineer and gunnery officers, drank damnation to the enemy.

Meanwhile, the *U-213*, her motors stopped, hung in the black depths, three hundred feet below the surface and an equal distance from the oozy black bottom.

It had been a successful hunt for the Kraken. Five porpoises, a small whale, and thousands of herring were digesting inside the great bag that was its stomach. With its eight sucker-lined tentacles folded complacently over the pink mouth of the bag, and its two long feelers thrown out in the current, just in case something in the way of dessert came along, the Kraken floated comfortably at a depth of some twenty fathoms.

Then, without warning, the great bag was suddenly constricted. The whale shot from the pink mouth like a discharged torpedo, followed immediately by the remains of the porpoises and a dark cloud that had been a school of herring. The ten serpentine arms writhed as the deflated bag twisted around the calcareous slab that served the Kraken as a skeleton.

Scarcely had the Kraken resumed his natural shape when that terrible, invisible force seized it again. Four times in all was the monster subjected to this weird *squeeze,* and the experience left it momentarily helpless and not a little afraid.

Twelve centuries had passed since the Kraken was spawned in the cold North Sea, a miniature of its present self, not one tenth as large as the smallest sucker disk on the newest tentacle. It was ten since the growing cephalopod, even then a giant among its race, had learned to seize those strange fish that swam only on the surface and pick off the tiny but delectable parasites that cluttered their backs. Fully two centuries ago the Kraken, stung painfully by these same queer fish, had abandoned the surface of the sea and taken to the quiet depths.

Even here, the monster now remembered, it had not always been safe. This was not the first time it had suffered from that invisible but none the less potent *squeeze*. But the sea offered only two realms: the surface and the depths. The Kraken had been driven from one. It determined to fight for the other.

With a flash of its broad fins that, stretching along each side of its bag-like stomach, made that vast appendage serve also in lieu of a body, the Kraken surged forward. Its two long feeler tentacles probed the darkness ahead, searching for this new enemy.

Diedrich lowered his glass to receive the report of a stocky *Bootsmannsmaat*. "No leaks, no plates strained, *Herr Kapitan*."

"Good," nodded the commander. "Not that I expected anything of the sort. Gentlemen, may trouble always avoid us by as wide a berth as the *Englander* depth bombs give us."

"Sinful," remarked von Rothberg. "Wasting all that money just to kill a few fish."

The others laughed and held out their glasses to the steward. But the amber liquor never reached them. Even as the man tilted the bottle, the *U-213* rolled heavily to port, then swung back in an arc that laid her on her beam ends. Men and gear were catapulted across the narrow chambers, and from the bow came a rumble and screams of agony. The gunnery officer was the first one to extricate himself from the tangle in the control chamber.

"A torpedo is loose," he cried, clambering awkwardly over the maze of pipes, wires, and valves that lined the submarine's sides. The next moment he was hurled into a corner, where his head hit a pipe with a sickening crunch.

The ship rolled faster, in ever lengthening arcs, while the crew tumbled about helplessly. Cries of pain and alarm echoed through the white steel tunnel, punctuated with the metallic clamor of tools and gear gone wildly adrift.

"Battle stations!" roared Diedrich, clawing to his feet. A rivulet of blood trickled down his face and disappeared into his golden beard, but the monocle still glittered in his right eye. "Secure all! Stand by to blow tanks!"

A warning siren cut through the clamor and men fought their way to their posts, where they clung desperately to anything that would afford a hand hold.

"Blow all tanks!"

Hissing and gurgling, the compressed air slowly forced the sea water out of the buoyancy tanks. Lightened, the *U-213* started to rise to the surface. But with her own increasing buoyancy and the lessening of the pressure, she rolled more and more violently. Her stern seemed held in a vise, but the bow threshed about wildly. The commander, eyeing the instruments, was frankly bewildered.

"Name of God, what is it?" cried von Rothberg.

Diedrich shook his head. The *U-213* was up to twenty fathoms and rising fast—but nowhere near as fast as she should. "Full ahead, both motors!" he barked.

Under the impetus of her twin screws, the *U-213* surged ahead. At once the violence of the rolling decreased, and the bow no longer whipped about like a charged wire.

"Up ship!" Diedrich commanded. Men sprang to the levers controlling the elevator planes and the submarine began to climb. Faster and faster moved the needle of the fathometer, until it read zero. The ship gave one final spurt and came down to an even keel with a bone-jarring crash.

"All clear on the surface," Diedrich muttered, revolving the periscope. "Surface battle stations! We'll see what was playing with us."

The hatch overhead clanged open and the commander, followed by his lieutenant and three seamen, two of whom carried an unmounted machine gun, climbed the steel ladder to the chariot bridge. While the seamen mounted the gun, the two officers scanned the choppy surface of the sea.

"Nothing!" growled von Rothberg. "Not a thing in sight. But what could have tossed us around? Submarine volcano eruption?"

"No," answered Diedrich. "Nothing like that. We'd have felt the heat. Did you notice, after the motors started, the ship hung for a moment, then leaped like a frightened hare? Something had hold of us."

The sea gave no answer. Except for half a dozen wheeling gulls, there was not another living thing in sight. Forward, a somewhat battered gun crew had the 105-millimeter rifle stripped for action and were looking grimly about for a target.

"Switch to the Diesels," Diedrich ordered. "No use running down our batteries." The humming of the electric motors ceased and the coughing of the surface engines took its place. Diedrich took the wheel and swung the *U-213* in a wide circle.

"We were going almost due north when we came up," he commented. "We'll backtrack a little. Maybe we'll raise something."

It was perhaps five minutes later that von Rothberg turned a puzzled face to his commander. "We seem to be slowing down," he said.

Diedrich turned from his search of the surface and shot a glance ahead. The bow wave was rapidly diminishing and what little there still was could be accounted for by the rising wind current. Aft there was a tremendous boil as the powerful screws bit into the solid water. The ship was beginning to vibrate.

"This is it," the commander said softly. "Look alive, now." His hand sought the engine-room telegraph and rang to "Stop." The vibration ceased and the ship rode easily.

"Gott im Himmel!"

The cry was wrung from one of the gunners forward. He stood up to his knees in the green water, seemingly rooted to a spot from which his comrades had retreated. The man cried aloud again, then whipped out his knife and stabbed viciously at something close to his legs.

"She's going down by the bow," the lieutenant cried, starting forward. "The gun platform's awash."

He had scarcely cleared the high bridge when the gunner, still screaming, was borne across the deck and disappeared into the water off the port side. His mates stood by dumbly.

"Grab him!" shouted the officer. "Do something! *Schnell!"*

Then von Rothberg, too, halted dumbly. Creeping across the tapering deck of the submarine were six immense tentacles, each as thick as a hundred-year oak. Slowly, deliberately they moved, three rising from each side of the ship. As the tips met and passed, like nothing so much as a monstrous, living claw, the deck dipped under their weight and green water poured through the open forward hatch.

"The hatch!" roared Diedrich from the bridge. "Close it!"

The command was unnecessary. Willing hands appeared from below and the steel hatch clanged shut. A series of muffled rings followed as the dogs were locked home.

A cry went up from the remaining gunners.

"*The Kraken! The Kraken!* We are lost."

"Swing that rifle around," ordered the commander. "Train it on those damned tentacles where they clear the ship. Rapid fire, if you value your lives."

From Diedrich's side came the chatter of the machine gun. A line of holes appeared along the nearest tentacle. But the beast under the ship minded them as little as a bull minds the scratch of a thorn bush. The tentacle quivered slightly, but did not pause in its course across the deck.

The rifle spat flame, and as the roar of the explosion rocked the men on the bridge they saw one of the six mighty arms whip into the air and fall limply into the sea. A cheer went up from the gunners as they rammed home another round. Again the big rifle spoke, and again a severed tentacle slithered back into the green sea.

"*Ausgucken!*"

Diedrich screamed the warning, but, deafened by the reports of the big rifle, the gunners failed to hear it. Another second and it was too late. The Kraken's two feeler tentacles, five times as long as its eight regular arms, had risen from the sea and hung over the exulting gun crew, the spatulate tips undulating. Then, striking with the speed of vipers, they scooped up the five men and pulled them under the surface.

By the now the great tentacles were seemingly endless loops thrown over the fore part of the slender hull. The immense weight of the monster, whose displacement

34

exceeded that of the *U-213* herself, was steadily pulling the submarine under.

"Prepare to dive!" groaned Diedrich.

The siren wailed in the bowels of the ship as the survivors dropped down the ladder. The water was already lapping at the chariot bridge as the commander, with a last despairing look forward, descended and closed the hatch.

"We can't fight that monster," he told the lieutenant, who was regarding him questioningly. "Not now, anyway, while it's clinging to the ship."

"Perhaps it will shift forward," von Rothberg said hopefully. "In front of the tubes. And then—"

"Are you a fool?" snapped Diedrich. "Would you explode a torpedo under our very bows? We might as well seek the depth bombs of the English."

In its present position the submarine was absolutely helpless. Its bow, under the weight of the Kraken, was submerged, while its stern stood clear of the surface.

"Flood the forward tanks," snapped Diedrich. "We'll try a crash dive. Maybe we can shake that *Teufel* off. Shades of the good Bishop Pontoppidan. He was not far wrong when he described the Kraken as being two kilometers across."

"You believe those superstitions, *Herr Kapitan?*" cried von Rothberg above the gurgling of the sea water.

"I believe my own eyes, *Leutnant,*" the older man snapped back. "Did you recognize that monster? It is a cuttlefish, a cephalopod. But the *Grosspapa* of them all. It must be hundreds of years old, if not a thousand. I'm afraid poor Heinkel, the gunner, was right. It *is* the Kraken."

"But the Kraken," insisted von Rothberg, "has not been reported in two hundred years. Be reasonable, *Herr Kapitan.* This is bad enough as it is."

" 'Reported,' no. But how do you know the monster has not been *sighted*? How many North Sea fishermen could engage this beast and return home to tell of it? What chance would a smack, or a trawler, even, have? Only our steel plates have saved *us*."

Von Rothberg would have protested further, but just then the U-boat's stern sank beneath the water and the screws took hold, driving the ship toward the bottom. Diedrich spun to his instruments, and signaled for the stern tanks to be flooded, to restore the ship's equilibrium when the Kraken had been shaken off.

As the Kraken bored through the depths, anger seethed along the few nerve threads that served the monster as a brain. It was not so much the pain of being squeezed— for, with its limited nervous system, the Kraken did not feel pain easily—but the loss of its dinner. It had been many years since the Kraken had dined so well. Those odd fish that swam on the surface, and which, long ago, drove him to the depths, were gobbling up the best of the schools. The Kraken knew this, because it had occasionally caught and crushed such fish and found tons of herring inside.

But still, the Kraken was not a natural fighter. Not since it had passed its hundredth birthday had it found it necessary to fight for its life. Nor, with its vast bulk and infinitesimal brain, was it easily aroused. Twenty-odd years before—it might have been yesterday to the Kraken —that strange but powerful *squeeze* had seized it. Sometimes its pressure was violent, sometimes merely annoying. The Kraken had almost forgotten it when it was caught again in the diamond-patterned quadruple explosion of the ash cans dumped on the *U-213*.

Had the Kraken found no enemy, the odds are that the monster would have gone on, seeking yet another dinner. But the submerged U-boat lay in its path.

The instant the Kraken's feelers contacted the cold steel hull they recoiled. Cautiously the Kraken advanced, until its huge globular eyes were focused on the motionless ship. It looked like a whale, but the Kraken knew very well it wasn't. No whale, even asleep, would allow its natural enemy to approach so closely. Around, over and under the stranger the Kraken swam. Then, becoming bolder, the monster shot out its feelers and seized the fluked tail. Still there was no sign of life. The Kraken drifted up to the ship, wrapped its many working arms around the tapering hull, and squeezed.

But the stranger ignored the pressure—a pressure which would have reduced a sperm whale to a pulp. It merely rolled under the Kraken's weight. Then, without warning, it came to life. Water spurted from its sides and it struggled toward the surface. Grimly the Kraken held onto its prize until the sea boiled in its face and forced it away.

Nothing daunted, the monster followed the stranger to the surface, where it started to swim away. Now the Kraken knew what it was: one of the odd fish that were so depleting its food supply. If so, there should be titbits, even if the fish itself was as indigestible as others of its kind. Flicking its immense fins, the Kraken followed, came up under the other and seized it again just behind the head. This time it would not escape.

Patiently the sucker disks crawled up and over the steel hull, tightening the grip of the mighty tentacles. As the tips of the serpentine arms looped back over the hull, the Kraken noticed one of the titbits it sought stuck to a sucker disk.

A silent gulp, and Kanoniersmaat Rudolph Himmler had paved the way for his shipmates.

The sudden loss of two tentacles startled the Kraken,

but only for a moment. Its appetite whetted by the remaining poor wretches scooped off the deck by its feelers, it renewed its efforts to subdue the big stranger. This time it was prepared for any sudden maneuver, and was not shaken off when the ship dove headlong toward the bottom.

Half an hour later the Kraken, swimming backward by expelling powerful jets of water from its gills, was towing the *U-213* to its subterranean den.

In the silent control chamber Korvettenkapitan Diedrich paced nervously, hands clasped behind his back and his bullet head thrust forward. Von Rothberg had found a seat and crouched over the *Schnapps* bottle, which, somehow, had remained unbroken. Forward in the torpedo room and aft in the engine room other men crouched, nursing pannikins of fiery rum issued by the commandant's order.

"There is nothing we can do. Nothing," Diedrich muttered. "It is suicide to go on deck while that monster has hold of the ship. We can only wait until it swims away. Perhaps then we may get a shot at it."

"What do you think happened to the gun crew?" the other asked.

"I prefer not to think," Diedrich snapped. He glanced at the chronometer. "It is now half an hour since we cut the motors and let that demon fish tow us where it will." He scanned the other instruments and the telltale tape that recorded their passage. "Nor'nor'east," he muttered, "at three knots. If this keeps up till midnight, we'll be in the Bukke Fjord."

Von Rothberg said nothing. He was regarding the bottle glumly. It was empty.

Hour after hour Diedrich kept his weary vigil. The air grew steadily fouler. It would have prostrated any but a veteran *Unterseeboot* sailor. Long before midnight the Kraken changed course and pointed almost due north, and Diedrich's hope that they might be rescued by one of the Norwegian gunboats based on Stavanger faded.

Then there was a scraping along the steel hull. It made a hellish clamor inside the ship and brought all hands to their feet. It stopped, then started again. Blows fell on the steel skin, and here and there a rivet started, sending a needle-thin stream shooting across the cluttered compartments.

A cry of alarm from the engine room turned Diedrich aft. "What's up?" he bellowed.

An oiler stumbled forward into the control chamber. "Both tail shafts snapped off, *Herr Kapitan*. Our propellers are gone. And water is coming through the packing boxes."

Diedrich glanced at the fathometer. It showed less than eight fathoms of water over them. A grating sound under his feet told him the ship was being dragged over the bottom.

"Blow all tanks!" he barked.

Von Rothberg came to life. "Easy, *Kapitan*," he warned. "We're in a tunnel of some sort. A cave."

"I guess as much," the commander said. "It would be the monster's den. But we will have to risk hitting the roof, or lose our keel, too."

Lightened, the *U-213* rode easier. There was less slamming and banging outside. But from the gyrations of the compass, it was evident they were following a twisting, turning course.

"Where are we?" von Rothberg wanted to know.

"Somewhere near, or under the Island of Karmo," Diedrich answered. "A little north of Skudeneshavn."

"Then we can call for help by radio."

"Yes," the commander conceded, "*if* we can't work ourselves out of this mess. I don't want the ship interned."

The keel grated along a pebbly bottom and the *U-213* came to rest. A check of the log tape told Diedrich the monster had towed them more than a hundred kilometers. Picking up the audiophone receiver, the commander listened intently. The faint swishing of the Kraken's long fins, which had haunted their passage, had ceased. He raised the periscope and looked around. It was pitch-black above.

"Rig a diver," he ordered, "and prepare the air lock. Equip him with an acetylene torch and a lamp."

A self-contained suit was dragged out of a locker, and a young torpedo man reluctantly wriggled into it.

"Now listen, Meyer," the commander told him. "I don't want you to take any unnecessary risks. Stick close to the air lock until you are sure the monster isn't around. There isn't much water here. You can blow to the surface using the periscope as a guide. There's a portable radio attached to that suit. Keep in constant communication with us."

"*Jawohl!*"

The face plate of the helmet was closed and locked, and willing arms guided the diver to the air lock.

"He's outside now," reported von Rothberg from the radio desk. "He's going aft." There was silence for a while. A circle of pale faces ringed von Rothberg. "He's under the stern," the lieutenant repeated. "Both screws gone and rudder unhoused. Now he's going up along the deck."

The leaden footsteps of the diver outside rang solemnly over the heads of the men inside the submarine. Unconsciously they looked up.

"He's going up," von Rothberg resumed. "His head is above the surface now. He says we're in a cavern.

40

Plenty of room on all sides and overhead. His light won't reach the—*Mein Gott!*"

Von Rothberg tore the headphones from his ears and looked up in horror. In the dead silence all could hear Meyer's muted screams:

"The Kraken!"

Recovering, the lieutenant replaced the headphones. "The monster has caught him," he told the white-faced, tense circle around him. "It's holding him high in the air."

"Tell the fool to use his torch," barked Diedrich.

"Use your torch on it, Meyer!" von Rothberg repeated. "Your torch, man!" He turned to Diedrich. "He's dropped it."

For a minute there was silence in the cold steel chamber. Then a shrill scream burst from the sensitive receivers. Involuntarily von Rothberg jerked them from his ears. In the tomblike quiet all could hear the doomed torpedo man's wail.

"It's swallowing me, *Herr Kapitan!* I am being devoured! Help! *Herr Kapitan! Herr Leutnant! Help!*"

The little circle broke up. The seamen and petty officers slumped to the cold deck and gave way to their emotions. Von Rothberg remained at the radio, the headphones clinging precariously to the back of his close-cropped head. Diedrich, his bearded face impassive and his arms folded across his chest, stood like a statue, the pale light glittering on his monocle. From time to time one of the others looked up at him hopefully.

Several minutes passed thus, then the headphones again stuttered. The lieutenant hastily shoved them back into place and listened intently. "Meyer's still alive," he reported. "He's in the monster's stomach. He still has his light."

Diedrich remained motionless. Not by a flicker of an

eyelash did he betray emotion. The men glanced at him and took their cue. Except for the sibilant breathing enforced by the foul air, the silence remained unbroken.

"He says it is like a monstrous cavern," von Rothberg continued. "The walls are a yellowish-white. . . . They sway back and forth. . . . They are lined with long white tendrils, like snakes. . . . He says the tendrils are reaching for him. . . . He's clinging to the wall, trying to cut his way out. . . . But it's hopeless. . . . There's a yellowish liquid seeping from the tips of the tendrils. . . . It is becoming foggy. . . . A drop of the liquid fell on his hand and burned. . . . He's afraid he will fall. . . . There's a pool of the liquid at the bottom of the stomach."

"That liquid would be mainly hydrochloric acid," Diedrich cut in. The commander's voice was controlled and icy, but von Rothberg, looking up, saw that his forehead was beaded with perspiration. "A creature of that size, and lacking teeth, would necessarily secrete a powerful digestive juice. Meyer is doomed, but fortunately he still has his knife."

Von Rothberg hesitated a moment and licked his dry lips. Then he spoke into the transmitter in a low voice. "You are lost, Meyer," he said. "We cannot help you. But you can die like a human being. Use your knife."

The lieutenant listened with bowed head. "He won't do it," he told Diedrich. "It is against his religion to commit suicide."

"It is an order."

The lieutenant repeated this. "The captain's order is that you kill yourself, Meyer. Now." There was another brief period of silence, during which von Rothberg's lips formed the word, "Praying."

Diedrich watched him stonily, and when the other jerked convulsively, he reached out and removed the headphones, dropping them on the radio desk. "Let the men have some air from the tanks," he said. "Not too much. And try to raise the home station."

The hissing of the compressed air tanks acted as a tonic on the crew. They came to life, but remained sitting or lying on their bunks. Von Rothberg, forcing the echoes of the unfortunate Meyer's dying cry from his mind, changed the wave length and hammered hopefully at the key.

"Well?" demanded the commander, after half an hour of this.

"No luck," responded the glum lieutenant. "There's a warship nearby. English. She's jamming our messages."

Diedrich swore roundly.

"Shall I try to raise the *Englander?*" von Rothberg asked. "Maybe they can get us out of here."

Diedrich shook his head. "No," he spat. "I won't give them the satisfaction of knowing we have fallen victim to a *verdammt Fisch*. Put a man on the audiophone. The Kraken will leave this den sometime. Then we will rise to the surface and look for a way out."

But it was two days before the Kraken left the cavern and swam through the water-filled tunnel to the open sea. During this time the crew of the *U-213* lay sprawled in a stupor, induced by liberal doses of veronal, laudanum, and whatever other soporifics the medicine chest offered. The practical-minded Diedrich, having no immediate use for them, and knowing that quiescent men require less oxygen, had chosen this way of conserving their dwindling supply of compressed air.

Diedrich, von Rothberg, the engineer officer, and the three senior petty officers, the only men remaining conscious, were sitting in the control chamber when the welcome swish of the monster's fins was heard on the audiophone. Diedrich immediately snatched the headphones from the radio man.

"It's going out, at last," he exulted. "The sounds are barely perceptible. But we'll wait till it's out of the tunnel."

It was a long wait for the impatient men. The tunnel, the commander had calculated from the telltale strips, was fully a mile long.

"All right now," he said finally. "Blow all tanks, easy."

Diedrich, as captain, opened the bridge hatch and was the first man outside. He sniffed cautiously. The air was musty and heavy with the odor of the sea and dead fish, but to men confined in a steel shell more than sixty hours, it was sweet. The remaining five climbed up after him and inhaled noisily.

"It will take that monster many hours, perhaps a full day, to feed," Diedrich said. "That will give us time to explore and if necessary, prepare a defense. Try the searchlight, *Leutnant*."

Von Rothberg swung the powerful beam in a complete circle. All around them was solid rock. There was no sign of the tunnel through which the *U-213* had been dragged.

"I was afraid of that," Diedrich said. "The tunnel mouth is under water. We'll have a devil of a time locating it. Search overhead."

The beam shot upward three hundred meters before it was reflected from the stone ceiling. Von Rothberg played it over the whole vast dome. There was no opening, no hint of one.

"There must be a vent somewhere," he told the commander. "This air is reasonably fresh."

"Take two men and the small boat and skirt the sides of this pool. You realize what it is, of course?"

"An ancient volcano?"

"Not exactly. Notice the folds in that rock. This stratum was forced up at some time and has subsequently

44

been excavated by the sea. You can see the marks of erosion. A general subsidence of the land carried the tunnel below sea level."

Several of the men below recovered consciousness and Diedrich turned them out. The rifle on the foredeck was cleaned and half a dozen rounds of high explosive shells were stacked beside it. The ship rode easily at anchor in the center of the pool. There was no place to moor her, and, anyway, Diedrich decided it would be safer to leave her where, if the Kraken should attack, she could not be slammed against anything harder than water.

"There's only one vent," von Rothberg reported on his return, "and it's entirely out of reach. Halfway to the top of the dome."

A groan went up from the others—with the exception of the iron commander. With the loss of her propellers the submarine was helpless, and their hopes had been based on finding a land exit from the cavern.

"We'll get out," Diedrich reassured them. "But first, we must kill this monster. We can do nothing while there's a danger that it will reappear."

Watches were resumed and the *U-213*'s crew settled down to await the return of the enemy. Big as the Kraken was, it could not survive half a dozen high explosive shells. A measure of confidence returned to the crew, and the older men began to relate stories of the underseas service in which crews had escaped from dangers as great, almost, as their own.

Diedrich was right in assuming that the Kraken would be busy a full day accumulating a dinner. It was not until three o'clock of the following morning that the monster signaled his approach on the audiophone. The crew immediately leaped to surface battle stations.

"It's taking its damned time," von Rothberg, standing beside the commander on the chariot bridge, muttered. Nervously he played the powerful beam over the still surface of the water.

"Shut off that light," Diedrich ordered suddenly. "It'll be shy of it and the beam will blind us. I've got a Very pistol. It's bound to splash when it gets into this shallow water."

The light winked out and the ten men—five at the rifle and five on the bridge—waited in utter darkness. Then the water rippled musically and a tiny wave washed against the steel side of the submarine. There was a muffled explosion as Diedrich fired a magnesium flare straight at the domed ceiling. The shell burst and unnaturally white light flooded the cavern.

"There it is. A point off the starboard bow," shouted the lieutenant. "Rapid fire!" Diedrich barked. He hung half over the steel rail, part of his keen brain taking in the grotesque monster threshing toward them, and the rest intent on another danger, almost as great, which he had foreseen, but which he had to risk.

The rifle roared, and the reverberations deafened them. Von Rothberg fired two more flares to give the gunners light. Again and again the big rifle spoke, but in that inclosed space it sounded like a continuous rumbling.

"Lower! Lower!" Diedrich shouted. "Under water! Aim for the body!" But he could not hear the words himself. The gunners, laughing madly in the ghastly light, were scoring direct hits on the giant, writhing tentacles, the only part of the huge cephalopod visible.

Neither Diedrich nor the others heard the first rocks fall, but as he had half expected something of the sort, he was the first to interpret the sudden swells that set the ship to rolling. He glanced aside and saw a column of water rise high into the air not ten feet off their beam. Slapping von Rothberg on the back to attract his attention, Diedrich framed the words:

"Cease firing!"

The lieutenant nodded, ran down the ladder and started forward, where the gunners, with fresh ammunition passed up from below, had resumed their bombardment of the Kraken. He had not taken three steps when a huge section of the stone roof, dropping like a plummet, wiped gun and crew from sight. The fore part of the hull tore loose at his feet, the tough steel cracking like an eggshell. He went up to his waist in water, then the remainder of the ship, freed of the heavy bow, but still weighted by the engines and batteries aft, rocked back, lifting the gaping wound clear of the surface. A sailor ran to his aid and dragged him back to the comparative security of the bridge.

"Unfortunate," Diedrich murmured. Only the lieutenant was in a position to read his lips.

Turning, von Rothberg glanced below. The stern was sinking, far deeper than the weight of the engines should have carried it. He slipped down the ladder. The floor of the control chamber stood at a forty-five-degree angle. Above him glowed the unholy light of the flare, where the whole forward end of the compartment lay open. Below him was the closed door leading to the engine room and the after compartments. Through the thick glass port set in it he saw water lapping. It was clear to him now. The stern had been stove in, and the shock of that mighty rock that tore off the bow had dislodged the door. It had swung shut, the dogs falling into place automatically.

"*Kapitan!*" he shouted. Then remembering the com-

47

mander was as deaf as himself, he crawled back up the ladder and caught him by the leg. Diedrich looked down and nodded.

They two, and the three sailors on the bridge, were the sole survivors. And they would not survive long.

Diedrich came down the ladder, followed by the sailors. The latter were popeyed with fright and twitching with fear. Diedrich opened the closet containing the self-contained diving rigs. There were seven left. They were not regulation equipment for submarines of the *U-213*'s class, but Diedrich had brought them in the hope of pulling off one of his many fantastic schemes—that of *carrying* a torpedo into an enemy naval base over the bottom. He now motioned for the others to don suits and got into one himself. Awkwardly, they dressed each other. Von Rothberg found that with the aid of the radio headphones they could converse, although the others' eardrums must have ruptured like his own.

"The Kraken is not dead yet," Diedrich told them. "I saw it swimming around. But it has lost all ten tentacles now and is comparatively helpless. It is my idea that it will head for the open sea to escape us."

"And we will follow it through the tunnel?" von Rothberg asked.

Diedrich smiled coldly through the glass face plate. "You forget, *Leutnant,* that the tunnel is more than a mile long. And only Father Neptune knows what kind of a bottom it has. No, I intend that the Kraken, who towed us in here, should tow us out."

He picked up a keen-edged harpoon from a locker, fitted it to a shaft and bent the end of a coil of light line to it. With the harpoon in his hand, he went back up the ladder. One of the sailors picked up the line and followed. Von Rothberg brought up the rear.

48

The commander gave them their instructions. "I'm going to harpoon this fish, and when it dives into the tunnel, you grab the line and go over. Inflate your suits so that you float clear of the bottom. Lieutenant von Rothberg will go first, then you, Hirsh, you, Mueller, and you, Rothner. I will bring up the rear. I caution you, it will be a terrible passage, but whoever lets go of the line will be lost. At my order, cast off and blow to the surface. The tide is flowing now and will wash us ashore."

Diedrich took one last look at his ship, then flexed his arm. It was awkward, hurling a harpoon hampered by a heavy canvas rig, but he would have no time later to get into one. For fully half an hour they waited there while the Kraken, a mere vast bulk of flesh now, threshed the surface. Then the monster drifted close to the ship. The keen blade glittered in the beam of a flashlight, which now provided the only illumination. Suddenly Diedrich's arm went back, then flashed forward, and the haft quivered in the mountainous gray body. The line hissed off the deck as the creature sounded. A minute and it whipped into the air, taut as a fiddle-string and stretching toward the far wall. Unceremoniously Diedrich flipped it into von Rothberg's hand and pushed him overboard. The others followed in quick succession, but there was barely two fathoms of line trailing behind the commander when he went over.

As Diedrich had warned, the trip was a nightmare. He was slammed from wall to wall until it took all his iron nerve and determination to hang on. Only the fact that he instinctively shoved his feet ahead of him, so the lead soles took the brunt of the shocks, kept the suit from being torn off his back. Then a comparatively soft object struck him and clung to him for a moment. Diedrich spun on his line like a deep-sea lead. The manila under his hands was rigid as an iron bar. A sudden terror overcame him. What if the line parted under the weight of this extra drag? He allowed his feet to swing back and kicked savagely. Then the object was whirled away by the current.

How long the passage took, Diedrich never knew. It might have been a minute, and it might have been an hour. But when he felt himself drawn downward, and the pressure increased, he knew they were free of the tunnel. He gave the order to let go and released the line himself. Like a balloon he shot toward the surface, until he remembered to jiggle the flutter valve with his chin and release the excess air in the suit. His ascent was slowed. Immediately he called the others. Only three voices answered.

"So *that* was what struck me in the tunnel," he thought. "Wonder which one?" But he did not ask. The others had their own troubles.

Eventually his helmet broke through the surface. He allowed the suit to fill until he was floating easily, but not head down. Overhead the stars twinkled and a bright moon shone. It was, Diedrich thought, the most glorious sight in the world.

Sometime later Diedrich felt himself being hauled out of the water. Strange hands twisted the globular helmet from his head and stripped the canvas suit from him. He looked up. A man, a sailor from his round cap, was bending over him. Two ribbons fluttered from the back of the cap, each a generous double-handbreadth.

"My men," Diedrich said. "Find them."

"*Jawohl, Herr Kapitan,*" the other answered. "We have already picked them up."

Diedrich closed his eyes for the first time in three days.

When he awoke, he was lying in a bunk between clean sheets. He looked around. It was an officer's room. From the pitching and rolling of the vessel, he knew it was a destroyer. He closed his eyes again. Sometime later a steward entered with a bowl of steaming broth. Diedrich wriggled into a sitting position and wolfed it.

When the steward left, an officer took his place. He, too, wore the three gold stripes of a *Korvettenkapitan*. He introduced himself as Hans von Wohl, commander of the destroyer, the *Baden,* on North Sea Patrol. Diedrich gave his own name and ship.

"You were reported lost," von Wohl said. "The *Englander* that sank you caught the ship's number. And then you were two days overdue. What happened? We tried to question your three men, but they're all raving lunatics. They can only babble about that mythological Kraken. We've got them strapped to bunks."

"Was there an officer among them?" Diedrich asked.

"No. All seamen."

So it had been von Rothberg who had let go in the tunnel. Diedrich's heart sank. In his own way, he had liked the young Junker. He stole a side glance at von Wohl. The latter's square face was stony.

Diedrich turned away to think. There were only Hirsh, Mueller, and Rothner, besides himself, left alive out of a crew of fifty-one. And they were "raving lunatics." Suddenly Diedrich knew he could not tell the truth. Had von Rothberg, an officer and a nobleman, survived to substantiate his story, it might have been different.

"The admiralty will want a report," von Wohl prompted.

"Yes, of course," Diedrich said. "I'm recovered enough to sit up and write."

"We guessed that you crawled through a torpedo tube and blew to the surface," von Wohl went on, "but where did you get the suits?"

"Requisitioned them at Cuxhaven. I had an idea, but never got a chance to try it out. If you will allow me—"

"Of course. Of course. Consider this room as your own. It's the executive officer's. The steward will supply you with whatever you want."

Von Wohl left and Diedrich pulled himself out of the bunk. It was agony to move; he was black and blue from head to foot. But he forced himself into his uniform, which, cleaned and pressed, was hanging in a locker. He found a pair of scissors and trimmed his beard. Then, with his monocle set firmly in his right eye, he surveyed himself.

"An undertaker couldn't lay me out better," he told himself.

He found paper and a pen on the desk. His report was brief. He described the sinking of the *U-213* by depth bombs at a point near where he had been picked up. All but the eight men in the control chamber were killed outright or drowned by the flooding of the forward and after compartments, he explained. After waiting nearly three days, and failing to raise another ship or the home station by radio, he said, he had conceived the idea of donning the suits, flooding the control chamber and blowing to the surface. Four of them, apparently, he went on, survived the ascent. The temporary insanity of the others he ascribed to the nerve-racking experience.

He read over the report. It was concise and logical. The admiralty would approve it and file it away with hundreds of others, and the matter would be ended.

Then, because the High Seas Fleet frowned on a captain who survived the loss of his ship and entire crew, he took the executive officer's pistol from the drawer and closed the incident.

III · THE DRAGON

In discussing dragons it must be made clear that there are two different species, which are very little alike. One is the Western dragon, the dragon of European fairy tales—a fierce, wicked, fire-breathing monster—a creature essentially evil, representing all that is most frightful, destructive, and terrifying in nature. The other is the Eastern dragon, generally of a kind and helpful nature—a gentle, benevolent creature, breathing mist instead of flame—a beast who bestows his wisdom and knowledge freely upon mankind.

The Western dragon reigns supreme among mythical monsters, possessing a majesty and power unique in animal lore. This dragon is at least as old as recorded history, but its appearance constantly changes, so it is not easy to describe. Most often it is portrayed as a winged reptile (the Eastern dragon rarely has wings), somewhat like a lizard in shape, usually but not always of enormous size, with a hideous, scaly body. The broad wings can be opened and closed, but it seldom uses them to fly. It haunts

53

remote places; rocky wilderness is its favorite retreat.

Edward Topsell, the seventeenth-century naturalist who wrote so vividly about all the beasts that were believed to exist in his time, describes the dragon in great detail in his *History of Four-Footed Beasts*.

Edward Topsell

THE GREATEST AMONG SERPENTS

Among all the kindes of Serpents, there is none comparable to the Dragon, or that affordeth and yeeldeth so much plentiful matter in History for the ample discovery of the nature thereof. . . .

There are divers sorts of Dragons, distinguished partly by their Countries, partly by their quantity and magnitude, and partly by the different form of their external parts. There be Serpents in *Arabia* called *Sirenae,* which have wings, being as swift as Horses, running or flying at their own pleasure, and when they wound a man, he dyeth before he feeleth pain. . . .

There are likewise other kinde of tame Dragons in *Macedonia,* where they are so meek, that women feed them, and suffer them to suck their breasts like little children; their Infants also play with them, riding upon them and pinching them, as they would do with Dogs, without any harm, and sleeping with them in their beds. . . .

[According to the verses of the poet Nicander] a Dragon is of a black colour, the belly somewhat green, and very beautiful to behold, having a treble row of teeth in their mouths upon every jaw, and with most bright and cleer seeing eyes, which caused the Poets to faign in their writings, that these Dragons are the watchfull keepers of the Treasures. They have also two dewlaps growing under their chin, and hanging down like a beard, which are of a red colour: their bodies are set all over with very sharp scales, and over their eyes stand certain flexible eye-lids. When they gape wide with their mouth, and thrust forth their tongue, their teeth seem very much to resemble the teeth of wilde Swine: And their necks have many times grosse thick hair growing upon them, much like unto the bristles of a wilde Boar.

Their mouth (especially of the most tameable Dragons) is but little, not much bigger than a pipe, through which they draw in their breath, for they wound not with their mouth, but with their tails, only beating with them when they are angry. But the *Indian, Aethiopian,* and *Phrygian* Dragons, have very wide mouths, through which they often swallow in whole fowls and beasts. Their tongue is cloven as if it were double, and the Investigators of nature do say, that they have fifteen teeth of a side. The males have combes on their heads, but the females have none, and they are likewise distinguished by their beards. . . .

Their meats are fruits and herbs, or any venomous creature, therefore they live long without food, and when they eat, they are not easily filled. They grow most fat by eating of egges, in devouring thereof they use this Art, if it be a great Dragon, he swalloweth it up whole, and then rowleth himself, whereby he crusheth the egges to pieces in his belly, and so nature casteth out the shells, and keepeth in the meat. But if it were a young Dragon, as if it be a Dragons whelp, he taketh the egge within the spire of his tail, and so crusheth it hard and holdeth it fast, untill his scales open the shell like a knife, then sucketh he out of the place opened all the meat of the egge. In like sort do the young ones pull off the feathers from the fowls which they eat, and the old ones swallow them whole, casting the feathers out of their bellies again. . . .

The Eastern dragon, a highly civilized creature, served a very important purpose in China: it was in charge of all the waterways, responsible for keeping the water pure and plentiful so that the crops would grow. Oriental dragons were fabulously rich, their treasures frequently including magical implements that brought miraculous power to their holders.

John Wyndham, the popular British science-fiction writer, tells an amusing story about one of these Oriental dragons.

John Wyndham

CHINESE PUZZLE

The parcel, waiting provocatively on the dresser, was the first thing that Hwyl noticed when he got in from work.

"From Dai, isn't it?" he inquired of his wife.

"Yes, indeed, Japanese the stamps are," she told him.

He went across to examine it. It was the shape a small hatbox might be, about ten inches each way perhaps. The address: Mr. & Mrs. Hwyl Hughes, Ty Derwen, Llynllawn, Llangolwgcoch, Brecknockshire, S. Wales, was lettered carefully, for the clear understanding of foreigners. The other label, also hand-lettered, but in red, was quite clear too. It said: EGGS—Fragile—With great CARE.

"There is funny to send eggs so far," Hwyl said. "Plenty of eggs we are having. Might be chocolate eggs, I think?"

"Come you to your tea, man," Bronwen told him. "All day I have been looking at that old parcel, and a little longer it can wait now."

Hwyl sat down at the table and began his meal. From time to time, however, his eyes strayed again to the parcel.

"If it is real eggs they are, careful you should be," he remarked. "Reading in a book I was once how in China they keep eggs for years. Bury them in the earth, they do, for a delicacy. There is strange for you, now. Queer they are in China, and not like Wales, at all."

Bronwen contented herself with saying that perhaps Japan was not like China, either.

When the meal had been finished and cleared, the parcel was transferred to the table. Hwyl snipped the string and pulled off the brown paper. Within was a tin box which, when the sticky tape holding its lid had been removed, proved to be full to the brim with sawdust. Mrs. Hughes fetched a sheet of newspaper and prudently covered the table top. Hwyl dug his fingers into the sawdust.

"Something there, there is," he announced.

"There is stupid, you are. Of course there is something there," Bronwen said, slapping his hand out of the way.

She trickled some of the sawdust out onto the newspaper, and then felt inside of the box herself. Whatever it was, it felt much too large for an egg. She poured out more sawdust and felt again. This time her fingers encountered a piece of paper. She pulled it out and laid it on the table: a letter in Dafydd's handwriting. Then she put in her hand once more, got her fingers under the object, and lifted it gently out.

"Well, indeed! Look at that now! Did you ever?" she exclaimed. "Eggs, he was saying, is it?"

They both regarded it with astonishment for some moments.

"So big it is. Queer, too," said Hwyl at last.

"What kind of bird to lay such an egg?" said Bronwen.

"Ostrich, perhaps?" suggested Hwyl.

But Bronwen shook her head. She had once seen an ostrich's egg in a museum, and remembered it well enough to know that it had little in common with this. The ostrich's egg had been a little smaller, with a dull, sallow-looking, slightly dimpled surface. This was smooth and shiny, and by no means had the same dead look: it had a luster to it, a nacreous kind of beauty.

"A pearl, could it be?" she said, in an awed voice.

"There is silly you are," said her husband. "From an oyster as big as Llangolwgcoch Town Hall, you are thinking?"

He burrowed into the tin again, but "Eggs," it seemed, had been a manner of speaking: there was no other, nor room for one.

Bronwen put some of the sawdust into one of her best vegetable dishes, and bedded the egg carefully on top of it. Then they sat down to read their son's letter:

S.S. Tudor Maid,
Kobe.

Dear Mam and Dad,

I expect you will be surprised about the enclosed I was too. It is a funny looking thing I expect they have funny birds in China after all they have Pandas so why not. We found a small sampan about a hundred miles off the China coast that had bust its mast and should never have tried and all except two of them were dead they are all dead now. But one of them that wasn't dead then was holding this egg-thing all wrapped up in a padded coat like it was a baby only I didn't know it was an egg then not till later. One of them died coming aboard but this other one lasted two days longer in spite of all I could do for him which was my best. I was sorry nobody here can speak Chinese because he was a nice little chap and lonely and knew he was a goner but there it is. And when he saw it was nearly all up he gave me this egg and talked very faint but I'd not have understood anyway. All I could do was take it and hold it careful the way he had and tell him I'd look after it which he couldn't understand either. Then he said something else and looked very worried and died poor chap.

So here it is. I know it is an egg because when I took him a boiled egg once he pointed to both of them to show me but nobody on board knows what kind of egg. But seeing I promised him I'd keep it safe I am sending it to you to keep for me as this ship is no place to keep anything safe anyway and hope it doesn't get cracked on the way too.

Hoping this finds you as it leaves me and love to all and you special

Dai

"Well, there is strange for you now," said Mrs. Hughes, as she finished reading. "And *looking* like an egg it is, indeed—the shape of it," she conceded. "But the colors are not. There is pretty they are. Like you see when oil is on the road in the rain. But never an egg like that have I seen in my life. Flat the color is on eggs, and not to shine."

Hwyl went on looking at it thoughtfully.

"Yes. There is beautiful," he agreed, "but what use?"

"Use, is it, indeed!" said his wife. "A trust, it is, and sacred, too. Dying the poor man was, and our Dai gave him his word. I am thinking of how we will keep it safe for him till he will be back, now."

They both contemplated the egg awhile.

"Very far away, China is," Bronwen remarked, obscurely.

Several days passed, however, before the egg was removed from display on the dresser. Word quickly went round the valley about it, and the callers would have felt slighted had they been unable to see it. Bronwen felt that continually getting it out and putting it away again would be more hazardous than leaving it on exhibition.

Almost everyone found the sight of it rewarding. Idris Bowen who lived three houses away was practically alone in his divergent view.

"The shape of an egg, it has," he allowed. "But careful you should be, Mrs. Hughes. A fertility symbol it is, I am thinking, and stolen, too, likely."

"Mr. Bowen—" began Bronwen, indignantly.

"Oh, by the men in that boat, Mrs. Hughes. Refugees from China they would be, see. Traitors to the Chinese people. And running away with all they could carry, before the glorious army of the workers and peasants could catch them, too. Always the same, it is, as you will be seeing when the revolution comes to Wales."

"Oh, dear, dear! There is funny you are, Mr. Bowen. Propaganda you will make out of an old boot, I think," said Bronwen.

Idris Bowen frowned.

"Funny I am not, Mrs. Hughes. And propaganda there is in an honest boot, too," he told her as he left with dignity.

By the end of a week practically everyone in the

village had seen the egg and been told no, Mrs. Hughes did not know what kind of a creature had laid it, and the time seemed to have come to store it away safely against Dafydd's return. There were not many places in the house where she could feel sure that it would rest undisturbed, but, on consideration, the airing-cupboard seemed as likely as any, so she put it back on what sawdust was left in the tin, and stowed it in there.

It remained there for a month, out of sight and pretty much out of mind until a day when Hwyl, returning from work, discovered his wife sitting at the table with a disconsolate expression on her face and a bandage on her finger. She looked relieved to see him.

"Hatched, it is," she observed.

The blankness of Hwyl's expression was irritating to one who had a single subject on her mind all day.

"Dai's egg," she explained. "Hatched out, it is, I am telling you."

"Well, there is a thing for you, now!" said Hwyl. "A nice little chicken, is it?"

"A chicken it is not, at all. A monster, indeed, and biting me it is, too." She held out her bandaged finger.

She explained that this morning she had gone to the airing-cupboard to take out a clean towel, and as she put her hand in, something had nipped her finger, painfully. At first she had thought that it might be a rat that had somehow got in from the yard, but then she had noticed that the lid was off the tin, and the shell of the egg there was all broken to pieces.

"How is it to see?" Hwyl asked.

Bronwen admitted that she had not seen it well. She had had a glimpse of a long, greeny-blue tail protruding from behind a pile of sheets, and then it had looked at her over the top of them, glaring at her from red eyes. On that, it had seemed to her more the kind of a job a man should deal with, so she had slammed the door and gone to bandage her finger.

"Still there, then, is it?" said Hwyl.

She nodded.

"Right you. Have a look at it, we will, now then," he said decisively.

He started to leave the room, but on second thoughts turned back to collect a pair of heavy work gloves. Bronwen did not offer to accompany him.

Presently there was a scuffle of his feet, an exclamation or two, then his tread descending the stairs. He came in, shutting the door behind him with his foot. He set the creature he was carrying down on the table, and for some seconds it crouched there, blinking, but otherwise un-moving.

"Scared, he was, I think," Hwyl remarked.

In the body, the creature bore some resemblance to a lizard—a large lizard, over a foot long. The scales of its skin, however, were much bigger, and some of them curled up and stood out here and there, in a finlike manner. And the head was quite unlike a lizard's, being much rounder, with a wide mouth, broad nostrils, and, over all, a slightly pushed-in effect, in which were set a pair of goggling red eyes. About the neck, and also making a kind of mane, were curious, streamer-like attachments with the suggestion of locks of hair which had permanently cohered. The color was mainly green, shot with blue and having a metallic shine to it, but there were brilliant red markings about the head and in the lower parts of the locks. There were touches of red, too, where the legs joined the body and on the feet, where the toes finished in sharp yellow claws. Altogether, a sur-prisingly vivid and exotic creature.

It eyed Bronwen Hughes for a moment, turned a

62

baleful look on Hwyl, and then started to run about the table top, looking for a way off. The Hugheses watched it for a moment or two, and then regarded one another.

"Well, there is nasty for you, indeed," observed Bronwen.

"Nasty it may be. But beautiful it is, too, look," said Hwyl.

"Ugly old face to have," Bronwen remarked.

"Yes, indeed. But fine colors, too, see. Glorious, they are, like technicolor, I am thinking," Hwyl said.

The creature appeared to have half a mind to leap from the table. Hwyl leaned forward and caught hold of it. It wriggled, and tried to get its head round to bite him, but discovered he was holding it too near the neck for that. It paused in its struggles. Then, suddenly, it snorted. Two jets of flame and a puff of smoke came from its nostrils. Hwyl dropped it abruptly, partly from alarm but more from surprise. Bronwen gave a squeal, and climbed hastily onto her chair.

The creature itself seemed a trifle astonished. For a few seconds it stood turning its head and waving the sinuous tail that was quite as long as its body. Then it scuttled across to the hearthrug, and curled itself up in front of the fire.

"By dammo! There was a thing for you!" Hwyl exclaimed, regarding it a trifle nervously. "Fire there was with it, I think. I will like to understand that, now."

"Fire indeed, and smoke, too," Bronwen agreed. "There is shocking it was, and not natural, at all."

She looked uncertainly at the creature. It had so obviously settled itself for a nap that she risked stepping down from the chair, but she kept on watching it, ready to jump up again if it should move. Then:

"Never did I think I will see one of those. And not

sure it is right to have in the house, either," she said.

"What is it you are meaning, now?" Hwyl asked, puzzled.

"Why, a dragon, indeed," Bronwen told him.

Hwyl stared at her.

"Dragon!" he exclaimed. "There is foolish—" Then he stopped. He looked at it again, and then down at the place where the flame had scorched his glove. "No, by dammo!" he said. "Right you. A dragon it is, I believe."

They both regarded it with some apprehension.

"Glad I am, not to live in China," observed Bronwen.

Those who were privileged to see the creature during the next day or two supported almost to a man the theory that it was a dragon. This they established by poking sticks through the wire netting of the hutch that Hwyl had made for it, until it obliged with a resentful huff of flame. Even Mr. Jones, the Chapel, did not doubt its authenticity, though on the propriety of its presence in his community he preferred to reserve judgment for the present.

After a short time, however, Bronwen Hughes put an end to the practice of poking it. For one thing, she felt responsible to Dai for its well-being, for another, it was beginning to develop an irritable disposition and a liability to emit flame without cause; for yet another, and although Mr. Jones's decision on whether it could be considered as one of God's creatures or not was still pending, she felt that in the meantime it deserved equal rights with other dumb animals. So she put a card on the hutch saying: PLEASE NOT TO TEASE, and most of the time was there to see that it was heeded.

Almost all Llynllawn, and quite a few people from Llangolwgcoch, too, came to see it. Sometimes they would stand for an hour or more, hoping to see it huff.

If it did, they went off satisfied that it was a dragon; but if it maintained a contented, non-fire-breathing mood, they went and told their friends that it was really no more than a little old lizard, though big, mind you.

Idris Bowen was an exception to both categories. It was not until his third visit that he was privileged to see it snort, but even then he remained unconvinced.

"Unusual, it is, yes," he admitted. "But a dragon it is not. Look you at the dragon of Wales, or the dragon of St. George, now. To huff fire is something, I grant you, but wings, too, a dragon must be having, or a dragon he is not."

But that was the kind of caviling that could be expected from Idris, and disregarded.

After ten days or so of crowded evenings, however, interest slackened. Once one had seen the dragon and exclaimed over the brilliance of its coloring, there was little to add, beyond being glad that it was in the Hughes's house rather than one's own, and wondering how big it would eventually grow. For really, it did not do much but sit and blink, and perhaps give a little huff of flame if you were lucky. So presently the Hughes's home became more their own again.

And, no longer pestered by visitors, the dragon showed an equable disposition. It never huffed at Bronwen, and seldom at Hwyl. Bronwen's first feeling of antagonism passed quickly, and she found herself growing attached to it. She fed it and looked after it, and found that on a diet consisting chiefly of minced horse-flesh and dog biscuits it grew with astonishing speed. Most of the time she let it run free in the room. To quiet the misgivings of callers she would explain:

"Friendly, he is, and pretty ways he has with him, if there is not teasing. Sorry for him, I am, too, for bad it is to be an only child, and an orphan worse still. And less than an orphan, he is, see. Nothing of his own sort he is knowing, nor likely, either. So very lonely he is being, poor thing, I think."

But inevitably, there came an evening when Hwyl, looking thoughtfully at the dragon, remarked:

"Outside you, soon. There is too big for the house you are getting, see."

Bronwen was surprised to find how unwilling she felt about that.

"Very good and quiet, he is," she said. "There is clever he is to tuck his tail away not to trip people, too. And clean with the house he is, also, and no trouble. Always out to the yard at proper times. Right as clockwork."

"Behaving well, he is, indeed," Hwyl agreed. "But growing so fast, now. More room he will be needing, see. A fine hutch for him in the yard, and with a run to it, I think."

The advisability of that was demonstrated a week later when Bronwen came down one morning to find the end of the wooden hutch charred away, the carpet and rug smoldering, and the dragon comfortably curled up in Hwyl's easy chair.

"Settled, it is, and lucky indeed not to burn in our bed. Out you," Hwyl told the dragon. "A fine thing to burn a man's house for him, and not grateful, either. For shame, I am telling you."

The insurance man who came to inspect the damage thought similarly.

"Notified, you should have," he told Bronwen. "A fire risk, he is, you see."

Bronwen protested that the policy made no mention of dragons.

"No, indeed," the man admitted, "but a normal

hazard he is not, either. Inquire, I will, from Head Office how it is, see. But better to turn him out before more trouble, and thankful, too."

So a couple of days later the dragon was occupying a larger hutch, constructed of asbestos sheets, in the yard. There was a wire-netted run in front of it, but most of the time Bronwen locked the gate and left the back door of the house open so that he could come and go as he liked. In the morning he would trot in and help Bronwen by huffing the kitchen fire into a blaze, but apart from that he had learned not to huff in the house. The only times he was any bother to anyone were the occasions when he set his straw on fire in the night so that the neighbors got up to see if the house was burning, and were somewhat short about it the next day.

Hwyl kept a careful account of the cost of feeding him, and hoped that it was not running into more than Dai would be willing to pay. Otherwise, his only worries were his failure to find a cheap, noninflammable bedding stuff, and speculation on how big the dragon was likely to grow before Dai should return to take him off their hands. Very likely all would have gone smoothly until that happened, but for the unpleasantness with Idris Bowen.

The trouble which blew up unexpectedly one evening was really of Idris' own finding. Hwyl had finished his meal and was peacefully enjoying the last of the day beside his door, when Idris happened along, leading his whippet on a string.

"Oh, hullo you, Idris," Hwyl greeted him amiably.

"Hullo you, Hwyl," said Idris. "And how is that phony dragon of yours, now then?"

"Phony, is it, you are saying?" repeated Hwyl, indignantly.

"Wings a dragon is wanting, to be a dragon," Idris insisted, firmly.

"Wings to hell, man! Come you and look at him now then, and please to tell me what he is if he is no dragon."

He waved Idris into the house, and led him through into the yard. The dragon, reclining in its wired run, opened an eye at them, then closed it again.

Idris had not seen it since it was lately out of the egg. Its growth impressed him.

"There is big he is now," he conceded. "Fine, the colors of him, and fancy, too. But still no wings to him, so a dragon he is not."

"What, then, is it he is?" demanded Hwyl.

How Idris would have replied to this difficult question was never to be known, for at that moment the whippet jerked its string free from his fingers, and dashed, barking, at the wire netting. The dragon was startled out of its snooze. It sat up suddenly, and snorted with surprise. There was a yelp from the whippet, which bounded into the air and then set off round and round the yard, howling. At last Idris managed to corner it and pick it up. All down the right side its hair had been scorched off, making it look very peculiar. Idris' eyebrows lowered.

"Trouble you want, is it? And trouble you will be having, by God!" he said.

He put the whippet down again, and began to take off his coat.

It was not clear whether he had addressed, and meant to fight, Hwyl or the dragon, but either intention was forestalled by Mrs. Hughes, coming to investigate the yelping.

"Oh! Teasing the dragon, is it!" she said. "There is shameful, indeed. A lamb the dragon is, as people know well. But not to tease. It is wicked you are, Idris Bowen, and to fight does not make right, either. Go you from here, now then."

Idris began to protest, but Bronwen shook her head and set her mouth.

"Not listening to you, I am, see. A fine brave man, to tease a helpless dragon. Not for weeks now has the dragon huffed. So go you, and quick."

Idris glowered. He hesitated, and pulled on his jacket again. He collected his whippet and held it in his arms. After a final disparaging glance at the dragon, he turned.

"Law I will have of you," he announced ominously, as he left.

Nothing more, however, was heard of legal action. It seemed as if Idris had either changed his mind or been advised against it, and that the whole thing would blow over. But three weeks later was the night of the Union Branch Meeting.

It had been a dull meeting, devoted chiefly to passing a number of resolutions suggested to it by its headquarters, as a matter of course. Then, just at the end, when there did not seem to be any other business, Idris Bowen rose.

"Stay, you!" said the chairman to those who were preparing to leave, and he invited Idris to speak.

Idris waited for persons who were half in and half out of their overcoats to subside, then:

"Comrades—" he began.

There was immediate uproar. Through the mingled approbation and cries of "Order" and "Withdraw" the chairman smote energetically with his gavel until quiet was restored.

"Tendentious, that is," he reproved Idris. "Please to speak halfway, and in good order."

Idris began again:

"Fellow workers. Sorry indeed, I am, to have to tell you of a discovery I am making. A matter of disloyalty, I am telling you: grave disloyalty to good friends and com— and fellow workers, see." He paused, and went on:

"Now every one of you is knowing of Hwyl Hughes's dragon, is it? Seen him for yourselves you have likely, too. Seen him myself, I have, and saying he was no dragon. But now then, I am telling you, wrong I was, wrong, indeed. A dragon he is, and not to doubt, though no wings.

"I am reading in the encyclopedia in Merthyr Public Library about two kinds of dragons, see. Wings the European dragon has, indeed. But wings the Oriental dragon has not. So apologizing now to Mr. Hughes, I am, and sorry."

A certain restiveness becoming apparent in the audience was quelled by a change in his tone.

"*But—*" he went on, "but another thing, too, I am reading there, and troubled inside myself with it, I am. I will tell you. Have you looked at the feet of this dragon, is it? Claws there is, yes, and nasty, too. But how many, I am asking you? And five, I am telling you. Five with each foot." He paused dramatically, and shook his head. "Bad, is that, bad indeed. For look you, Chinese is a five-toed dragon is, yes—but five-toed is not a Republican dragon, five-toed is not a People's dragon; five-toed is an *Imperial* dragon, see. A symbol, it is, of the oppression of Chinese workers and peasants. And shocking to think that in our village we are keeping such an emblem. What is it that the free people of China will be saying of Llynllawn when they will hear of this, I am asking? What is it Mao Tse-tung, glorious leader of the heroic Chinese people in their magnificent fight for peace, will be thinking of South Wales and this imperialist dragon—?" he was continuing, when differences of view in the audience submerged his voice.

Again the chairman called the meeting to order. He offered Hwyl the opportunity to reply, and after the situation had been briefly explained, the dragon was, on a show of hands, acquitted of political implication by all but Idris' doctrinaire faction, and the meeting broke up.

Hwyl told Bronwen about it when he got home.

"No surprise there," she said. "Jones the Post is telling me, telegraphing Idris has been."

"Telegraphing?" inquired Hwyl.

"Yes, indeed. Asking the *Daily Worker,* in London, how is the party line on imperialist dragons, he was. But no answer yet, though."

A few mornings later the Hugheses were awakened by a hammering on their door. Hwyl went to the window and found Idris below. He asked what the matter was.

"Come you down here, and I will show you," Idris told him.

After some argument, Hwyl descended. Idris led the way round to the back of his own house, and pointed.

"Look you there, now," he said.

The door of Idris' henhouse was hanging by one hinge. The remains of two chickens lay close by. A large quantity of feathers was blowing about the yard.

Hwyl looked at the henhouse more closely. Several deep-raked scores stood out white on the creosoted wood. In other places there were darker smears where the wood seemed to have been scorched. Silently Idris pointed to the ground. There were marks of sharp claws, but no imprint of a whole foot.

"There is bad. Foxes, is it?" inquired Hwyl.

Idris choked slightly.

"Foxes, you are saying. Foxes, indeed! What will it be but your dragon? And the police to know it, too."

Hwyl shook his head.

"No," he said.

"Oh," said Idris. "A liar, I am, is it? I will have the guts from you, Hwyl Hughes, smoking hot, too, and glad to do it."

"You talk too easy, man," Hwyl told him. "Only now the dragon is still fast in his hutch, I am saying. Come you now, and see."

They went back to Hwyl's house. The dragon was in his hutch, sure enough, and the door of it was fastened with a peg. Furthermore, as Hwyl pointed out, even if he had left it during the night, he could not have reached Idris' yard without leaving scratches and traces on the way, and there were none to be found.

They finally parted in a state of armistice. Idris was by no means convinced, but he was unable to get round the facts, and not at all impressed with Hwyl's suggestion that a practical joker could have produced the effect on the henhouse with a strong nail and a blowtorch.

Hwyl went upstairs again to finish dressing.

"There is funny it is, all the same," he observed to Bronwen. "Not seeing, that Idris was, but scorched the peg is, on the *outside* of the hutch. And how should that be, I wonder?"

"Huffed four times in the night the dragon has, five, perhaps," Bronwen said. "Growling, he is, too, and banging that old hutch about. Never have I heard him like that before."

"There is queer," Hwyl said, frowning. "But never out of his hutch, and that to swear to."

Two nights later Hwyl was awakened by Bronwen shaking his shoulder.

"Listen, now then," she told him.

There was an unmistakable growling going on at the back of the house, and the sound of several snorts.

"Huffing, he is, see," said Bronwen, unnecessarily.

There was a crash of something thrown with force, and the sound of a neighbor's voice cursing. Hwyl reluctantly decided that he had better get up and investigate.

Everything in the yard looked as usual, except for the presence of a large tin can which was clearly the object thrown. There was, however, a strong smell of burning, and a thudding noise, recognizable as the sound of the dragon tramping round and round in his hutch to stamp out the bedding caught alight again. Hwyl went across and opened the door. He raked out the smoldering straw, fetched some fresh, and threw it in.

"Quiet, you," he told the dragon. "More of this, and the hide I will have off you, slow and painful, too. Bed, now then, and sleep."

He went back to bed himself, but it seemed as if he had only just laid his head on the pillow when it was daylight, and there was Idris Bowen hammering on the front door again.

Idris was more than a little incoherent, but Hwyl gathered that something further had taken place at his house, so he slipped on jacket and trousers, and went down. Idris led the way down beside his own house, and threw open the yard door with the air of a conjurer. Hwyl stared for some moments without speaking.

In front of Idris' henhouse stood a kind of trap, roughly contrived of angle iron and wire netting. In it, surrounded by chicken feathers and glaring at them from eyes like live topazes, sat a creature, blood-red all over.

"Now, there is a dragon for you, indeed," Idris said. "Not to have colors like you see on a merry-go-round at a circus, either. A serious dragon, that one, and proper—wings, too, see?"

Hwyl went on looking at the dragon without a word. The wings were folded at present, and the cage did not give room to stretch them. The red, he saw now, was darker on the back and brighter beneath, giving it the rather ominous effect of being lit from below by a blast-furnace. It certainly had a more practical aspect than his own dragon, and a fiercer look about it altogether. He stepped forward to examine it more closely.

"Careful, man," Idris warned him, laying a hand on his arm.

The dragon curled back its lips, and snorted. Twin flames a yard long shot out of its nostrils. It was a far better huff than the other dragon had ever achieved. The air was filled with a strong smell of burnt feathers.

"A fine dragon, that is," Idris said again. "A real Welsh dragon for you. Angry he is, see, and no wonder. A shocking thing for an imperialist dragon to be in his country. Come to throw him out, he has, and mincemeat he will be making of your namby-pamby, best-parlor dragon, too."

"Better for him not to try," said Hwyl, stouter in word than heart.

"And another thing, too. Red this dragon is, and so a real People's dragon, see."

"Now then. Now then. Propaganda with dragons again, is it? Red the Welsh dragon has been two thousand years, and a fighter, too, I grant you. But a fighter for Wales, look; not just a loudmouth talker of fighting for peace, see. If it is a good red Welsh dragon he is, then out of some kind of egg laid by your Uncle Joe, he is not; and thankful, too, I think," Hwyl told him. "And look you," he added as an afterthought, "this one it is who is stealing your chickens, not mine, at all."

74

"Oh, let him have the old chickens, and glad," Idris said. "Here he is come to chase a foreign imperialist dragon out of his rightful territory, and a proper thing it is, too. None of your D.P. dragons are we wanting round Llynllawn, or South Wales, either."

"Get you to hell, man," Hwyl told him. "Sweet-dispositioned my dragon is, no bother to anyone, and no robber of henhouses, either. If there is trouble at all, the law I will be having of you and your dragon for disturbing of the peace, see. So I am telling you. And goodbye, now."

He exchanged another glance with the angry-looking, topaz eyes of the red dragon, and then stalked away, back to his own house.

That evening, just as Hwyl was sitting down to his meal, there was a knock at the front door. Bronwen went to answer it, and came back.

"Ivor Thomas and Dafydd Ellis wanting you. Something about the Union," she told him.

He went to see them. They had a long and involved story about dues that seemed not to have been fully paid. Hwyl was certain that he was paid-up to date, but they remained unconvinced. The argument went on for some time before, with headshaking and reluctance, they consented to leave. Hwyl returned to the kitchen. Bronwen was waiting, standing by the table.

"Taken the dragon off, they have," she said flatly.

Hwyl stared at her. The reason why he had been kept at the front door in pointless argument suddenly came to him. He crossed to the window and looked out. The back fence had been pushed flat, and a crowd of men carrying the dragon's hutch on their shoulders was already a hundred yards beyond it. Turning round, he saw Bronwen standing resolutely against the back door.

"Stealing, it is, and you not calling," he said accusingly.

"Knocked you down, they would, and got the dragon just the same," she said. "Idris Bowen and his lot, it is."

Hwyl looked out of the window again.

"What to do with him, now then?" he asked.

"Dragon fight, it is," she told him. "Betting, they were. Five to one on the Welsh dragon, and sounding very sure, too."

Hwyl shook his head.

"Not to wonder, either. There is not fair, at all. Wings, that Welsh dragon has, so air attacks he can make. Unsporting, there is, and shameful indeed."

He looked out of the window again. More men were joining the party as it marched its burden across the waste ground, toward the slag heap. He sighed.

"There is sorry I am for our dragon. Murder it will be, I think. But go and see it, I will. So no tricks from that Idris to make a dirty fight dirtier."

Bronwen hesitated.

"No fighting for you? You promise me?" she said.

"Is it a fool I am, girl, to be fighting fifty men, and more? Please to grant me some brains, now."

She moved doubtfully out of his way, and let him open the door. Then she snatched up a scarf and ran after him, tying it over her head as she went.

The crowd that was gathering on a piece of flat ground near the foot of the slag heap already consisted of something more like a hundred men than fifty, and there were more hurrying to join it. Several self-constituted stewards were herding people back to clear an oval space. At one end of it was the cage in which the red dragon crouched huddled, with a bad-tempered look. At the other, the asbestos hutch was set down, and its bearers withdrew. Idris noticed Hwyl and Bronwen as they came up.

"And how much is it you are putting on your dragon?" he inquired, with a grin.

Bronwen said, before Hwyl could reply:

"Wicked, it is, and shamed you should be, Idris Bowen. Clip you your dragon's wings to fight fair, and we will see. But betting against a horseshoe in the glove, we are not." And she dragged Hwyl away.

All about the oval the laying of bets went on, with the Welsh dragon gaining favor all the time. Presently, Idris stepped out into the open and held up his hands for quiet.

"Sport it is for you tonight. Supercolossal attractions as they are saying in the movies, and never again, likely. So put you your money, now. When the English law is hearing of this, no more dragon-fighting, it will be—like no more to cockfight." A boo went up, mingled with the laughter of those who knew a thing or two about cock-fighting that the English law did not. Idris went on: "So now the dragon championship, I am giving you. On my right, the Red Dragon of Wales, on his home ground. A People's dragon, see. For more than a coincidence, it is, that the color of the Welsh dragon—" His voice was lost for some moments in controversial shouts. It reemerged, saying: "—left, the decadent dragon of the imperialist exploiters of the suffering Chinese people, who, in their glorious fight for peace under the heroic leadership—" But the rest of his introduction was also lost among the catcalls and cheers that were still continuing when he beckoned forward attendants from the ends of the oval, and withdrew.

At one end, two men reached up with a hooked pole, pulled over the contraption that enclosed the red dragon, and ran back hurriedly. At the far end, a man knocked the peg from the asbestos door, pulled it open, scuttled behind the hutch and no less speedily out of harm's way.

The red dragon looked round, uncertainly. It tentatively tried unfurling its wings. Finding that possible, it reared up on its hind legs, supporting itself on its tail, and flapped its pinions energetically, as though to dispel the creases.

The other dragon ambled out of its hutch, advanced a few feet, and stood blinking. Against the background of the waste ground and the slag heap it looked more than usually exotic. It yawned largely, with a fine display of fangs, rolled its eyes hither and thither, and then caught sight of the red dragon.

Simultaneously, the red dragon noticed the other. It stopped flapping and dropped to all four feet. The two regarded one another. A hush came over the crowd. Both dragons remained motionless, except for a slight waving of the last foot or so of their tails.

The oriental dragon turned its head a little on one side. It snorted slightly, and shriveled up a patch of weeds.

The red dragon stiffened. It suddenly adopted a pose gardant, one forefoot uplifted, with claws extended, wings raised. It huffed with vigor, vaporized a puddle, and disappeared momentarily in a cloud of steam. There was an anticipatory murmur from the crowd.

The red dragon began to pace round, circling the other, giving a slight flap of its wings now and then.

The crowd watched it intently. So did the other dragon. It did not move from its position, but turned as the red dragon circled, keeping its head and gaze steadily toward it.

With the circle almost completed, the red dragon halted. It extended its wings widely, and gave a full-throated roar. Simultaneously, it gushed two streams of fire and belched a small cloud of black smoke. The part of the crowd nearest to it moved back, apprehensively.

At this tense moment Bronwen Hughes began suddenly to laugh. Hwyl shook her by the arm.

"Hush, you! There is not funny, at all," he said, but she did not stop at once.

The oriental dragon did nothing for a moment. It appeared to be thinking the matter over. Then it turned swiftly round, and began to run. The crowd behind it raised a jeer, those in front waved their arms to shoo it back. But the dragon was unimpressed by arm-waving. It came on, with now and then a short spurt of flame from its nostrils. The people wavered, and then scattered out of its way. Half a dozen men started to chase after it with sticks, but soon gave up. It was traveling at twice the pace they could run.

With a roar, the red dragon leaped into the air and came across the field, spitting flames like a strafing aircraft. The crowd scattered still more swiftly, tumbling over itself as it cleared a way.

The running dragon disappeared round the foot of the slag heap, with the other hovering above it. Shouts of disappointment rose from the crowd, and a good part of it started to follow, to be in at the death.

But in a minute or two the running dragon came into view again. It was making a fine pace up the mountainside, with the red dragon still flying a little behind it. Everybody stood watching it wind its way up and up until, finally, it disappeared over the shoulder. For a moment the flying dragon still showed as a black silhouette above the skyline, then, with a final whiff of flame, it, too, disappeared—and the arguments about paying up began.

Idris left the wrangling to come across to the Hugheses.

"So there is a coward your imperialist dragon is, then. And not one good huff, or a bite to him, either," he said.

Bronwen looked at him, and smiled.

"So foolish you are, Idris Bowen, with your head full of propaganda and fighting. Other things than to fight, there is, even for dragons. Such a brave show your red dragon was making, such a fine show, oh yes—and very like a peacock, I am thinking. Very like the boys in their Sunday suits in Llangolwgcoch High Street, too—all dressed up to kill, but not to fight."

Idris stared at her.

"And our dragon," she went on. "Well, there is not a very new trick, either. Done a bit of it before now, I have, myself." She cast a sidelong glance at Hwyl.

Light began to dawn on Idris.

"But—but it is *he* you were always calling your dragon," he protested.

Bronwen shrugged.

"Oh, yes, indeed. But how to tell with dragons?" she asked.

She turned to look up the mountain.

"There is lonely, lonely the red dragon must have been these two thousand years—so not much bothering with your politics, he is, just now. More single with his mind, see. And interesting it will be, to be having a lot of baby dragons in Wales before long, I am thinking."

We are all familiar with the legend of St. George and the dragon—how the hero pitted his strength and courage against that of a terrible creature with breath of flames and heart of evil. This legend usually ends with St. George slaying the dragon and so bringing peace to the land. Kenneth Grahame, author of the beloved *The Wind in the Willows,* puts a new twist to this old tale in the amusing story that follows.

Kenneth Grahame

THE RELUCTANT DRAGON

Long ago—might have been hundreds of years ago—in a cottage half-way between this village and yonder shoulder of the Downs up there, a shepherd lived with his wife and their little son. Now the shepherd spent his days—and at certain times of the year his nights too—up on the wide ocean-bosom of the Downs, with only the sun and the stars and the sheep for company, and the friendly chattering world of men and women far out of sight and hearing. But his little son, when he wasn't helping his father, and often when he was as well, spent much of his time buried in big volumes that he borrowed from the affable gentry and interested persons of the country round about. And his parents were very fond of him, and rather proud of him too, though they didn't let on in his hearing, so he was left to go his own way and read as much as he liked; and instead of frequently getting a cuff on the side of the head, as might very well have happened to him, he was treated more or less as an equal by his parents, who sensibly thought it a very fair division of labour that they should supply the practical knowledge, and he the book-learning. They knew that book-learning often came in useful at a pinch, in spite of what their neighbors said. What the boy chiefly dabbled in was natural history and fairy-tales, and he just took them as they came, in a sandwichy sort of way, without making any distinctions; and really his course of reading strikes one as rather sensible.

One evening the shepherd, who for some nights past had been disturbed and preoccupied, and off his usual mental balance, came home all of a tremble, and, sitting down at the table where his wife and son were peacefully employed, she with her seam, he in following out the adventures of the Giant with no Heart in his Body, exclaimed with much agitation:

"It's all up with me, Maria! Never no more can I go up on them there Downs, was it ever so!"

"Now don't you take on like that," said his wife, who was a *very* sensible woman; "but tell us all about it first, whatever it is as has given you this shake-up, and then me and you and the son here, between us, we ought to be able to get to the bottom of it!"

"It began some nights ago," said the shepherd. "You know that cave up there—I never liked it, somehow, and the sheep never liked it neither, and when sheep don't like a thing there's generally some reason for it. Well, for some time past there's been faint noises coming from that cave—noises like heavy sighings, with grunts mixed up in them; and sometimes a snoring, far away down— *real* snoring, yet somehow not *honest* snoring, like you and me o'nights, you know!"

"*I* know," remarked the boy quietly.

"Of course I was terrible frightened," the shepherd went on; "yet somehow I couldn't keep away. So this very evening, before I come down, I took a cast round by the cave, quietly. And there—O Lord!—there I saw him at last, as plain as I see you!"

"Saw *who?*" said his wife, beginning to share in her husband's nervous terror.

"Why *him*, I'm a-telling you!" said the shepherd. "He was sticking half-way out of the cave, and seemed to be enjoying of the cool of the evening in a poetical sort of way. He was as big as four cart-horses, and all covered with shiny scales—deep-blue scales at the top of him, shading off to a tender sort o' green below. As he breathed, there was that sort of flicker over his nostrils that you see over our chalk roads on a baking, windless day in summer. He had his chin on his paws, and I should say he was meditating about things. Oh yes, a peaceable sort o' beast enough, and not ramping or carrying on or doing anything but what was quite right and proper. I admit all that. And yet, what am I to do? *Scales,* you know, and claws, and a tail for certain, though I didn't see that end of him—I ain't *used* to 'em, and I don't *hold* with 'em, and that's a fact!"

The boy, who had apparently been absorbed in his book during his father's recital, now closed the volume, yawned, clasped his hands behind his head, and said sleepily:

"It's all right, Father. Don't you worry. It's only a dragon."

"Only a dragon?" cried his father. "What do you mean, sitting there, you and your dragons? *Only* a dragon indeed! And what do *you* know about it?"

" 'Cos it *is,* and 'cos I *do* know," replied the boy quietly. "Look here, Father, you know we've each of us got our line. *You* know about sheep and weather and things; *I* know about dragons. I always said, you know, that that cave up there was a dragon-cave. I always said it must have belonged to a dragon some time, and ought to belong to a dragon now, if rules count for anything. Well, now you tell me it *has* got a dragon, and so *that's* all right. I'm not half as much surprised as when you told me it *hadn't* got a dragon. Rules always come right if you wait quietly. Now, please, just leave this all to me. And I'll stroll up to-morrow morning—no, in the morning I can't, I've got a whole heap of things to do—well, perhaps in the evening, if I'm quite free, I'll go up and have a talk to him, and you'll find it'll be all right. Only, please, don't you go worrying round there without me. You don't understand 'em a bit, and they're very sensitive, you know!"

"He's quite right, Father," said the sensible mother. "As he says, dragons is his line and not ours. He's wonderful knowing about book-beasts, as everyone allows. And to tell the truth, I'm not half happy in my own mind, thinking of that poor animal lying alone up there, without a bit o' hot supper or anyone to change the news with; and maybe we'll be able to do something for him; and if he ain't quite respectable our boy'll find it out quick enough. He's got a pleasant sort o' way with him that makes everybody tell him everything."

Next day, after he'd had his tea, the boy strolled up the chalky track that led to the summit of the Down; and there, sure enough, he found the dragon, stretched lazily on the sward in front of his cave. The view from that point was a magnificent one. To the right and left, the bare and billowy leagues of Downs; in front, the vale, with its clustered homesteads, its threads of white roads running through orchards and well-tilled acreage, and, far away, a tint of grey old cities on the horizon. A cool breeze played over the surface of the grass, and the silver shoulder of a large moon was showing above distant junipers. No wonder the dragon seemed in a peaceful and contented mood; indeed, as the boy approached he could hear the beast purring with a happy regularity. "Well, we live and learn!" he said to himself. "None of my books ever told me that dragons purred!"

"Hallo, Dragon!" said the boy quietly, when he had got up to him.

The dragon, on hearing the approaching footsteps, made the beginning of a courteous effort to rise. But when he saw it was a boy, he set his eyebrows severely.

"Now don't you hit me," he said; "or bung stones, or squirt water, or anything. I won't have it, I tell you!"

"Not goin' to hit you," said the boy wearily, dropping on the grass beside the beast; "and don't, for goodness' sake, keep on saying 'Don't'; I hear so much of it, and it's monotonous, and makes me tired. I've simply looked in to ask you how you were and all that sort of thing; but if I'm in the way I can easily clear out. I've lots of friends, and no one can say I'm in the habit of shoving myself in where I'm not wanted!"

"No, no, don't go off in a huff," said the dragon hastily; "fact is, I'm as happy up here as the day's long; never without an occupation, dear fellow, never without an occupation! And yet, between ourselves, it *is* a trifle dull at times."

The boy bit off a stalk of grass and chewed it. "Going to make a long stay here?" he asked politely.

"Can't hardly say at present," replied the dragon. "It seems a nice place enough—but I've only been here a short time, and one must look about and reflect and con-sider before settling down. It's rather a serious thing, settling down. Besides—now I'm going to tell you some-thing! You'd never guess it if you tried ever so!—fact is, I'm such a confounded lazy beggar!"

"You surprise me," said the boy civilly.

"It's the sad truth," the dragon went on, settling down between his paws and evidently delighted to have found a listener at last; "and I fancy that's really how I came to be here. You see, all the other fellows were so active and *earnest* and all that sort of thing—always rampaging and skirmishing and scouring the desert sands, and pacing the margin of the sea, and chasing knights all over the place, and devouring damsels, and going on generally— whereas I liked to get my meals regular and then to prop my back against a bit of rock and snooze a bit, and wake up and think of things going on and how they kept going on just the same, you know! So when it happened I got fairly caught."

"When *what* happened, please?" asked the boy.

85

"That's just what I don't precisely know," said the dragon. "I suppose the earth sneezed, or shook itself, or the bottom dropped out of something. Any how there was a shake and a roar and a general stramash, and I found myself miles away underground and wedged in as tight as tight. Well, thank goodness, my wants are few, and at any rate I had peace and quietness and wasn't always being asked to come along and *do* something. And I've got such an active mind—always occupied, I assure you! But time went on, and there was a certain sameness about the life, and at last I began to think it would be fun to work my way upstairs and see what you other fellows were doing. So I scratched and burrowed, and worked this way and that way and at last I came out through this cave here. And I like the country and the view and the people—what I've seen of 'em—and on the whole I feel inclined to settle down here."

"What's your mind always occupied about?" asked the boy. "That's what I want to know."

The dragon coloured slightly and looked away. Presently he said bashfully:

"Did you ever—just for fun—try to make up poetry—verses, you know?"

" 'Course I have," said the boy. "Heaps of it. And some of it's quite good, I feel sure, only there's no one here cares about it. Mother's very kind and all that, when I read it to her, and so's father for that matter. But somehow they don't seem to—"

"Exactly," cried the dragon; "my own case exactly. They don't seem to, and you can't argue with 'em about it. Now you've got culture, you have, I could tell it on you at once, and I should just like your candid opinion about some little things I threw off lightly, when I was down there. I'm awfully pleased to have met you, and

I'm hoping the other neighbours will be equally agreeable. There was a very nice old gentleman up here only last night, but he didn't seem to want to intrude."

"That was my father," said the boy, "and he *is* a nice old gentleman, and I'll introduce you some day if you like."

"Can't you two come up here and dine or something to-morrow?" asked the dragon eagerly. "Only, of course, if you've got nothing better to do," he added politely.

"Thanks awfully," said the boy, "but we don't go out anywhere without my mother, and, to tell you the truth, I'm afraid she mightn't quite approve of you. You see, there's no getting over the hard fact that you're a dragon, is there? And when you talk of settling down, and the neighbours, and so on, I can't help feeling that you don't quite realize your position. You're an enemy of the human race, you see!"

"Haven't got an enemy in the world," said the dragon cheerfully. "Too lazy to make 'em, to begin with. And if I *do* read other fellows my poetry, I'm always ready to listen to theirs!"

"Oh dear!" cried the boy, "I wish you'd try and grasp the situation properly. When the other people find you out, they'll come after you with spears and swords and all sorts of things. You'll have to be exterminated, according to their way of looking at it! You're a scourge and a pest and a baneful monster!"

"Not a word of truth in it," said the dragon, wagging his head solemnly. "Character'll bear the strictest investigation. And now, there's a little sonnet-thing I was working on when you appeared on the scene—"

"Oh, if you *won't* be sensible," cried the boy, getting up, "I'm going off home. No, I can't stop for sonnets; my mother's sitting up. I'll look you up to-morrow, some time or other, and do for goodness' sake try and realize that you're a pestilential scourge, or you'll find yourself in a most awful fix. Good night!"

The boy found it an easy matter to set the mind of his parents at ease about his new friend. They had always left that branch to him, and they took his word without a murmur. The shepherd was formally introduced and many compliments and kind inquiries were exchanged. His wife, however, though expressing her willingness to do anything she could—to mend things, or set the cave to rights, or cook a little something when the dragon had been poring over sonnets and forgotten his meals, as male things *will* do—could not be brought to recognize him formally. The fact that he was a dragon and "they didn't know who he was" seemed to count for everything with her. She made no objection, however, to her little son spending his evenings with the dragon quietly, so long as he was home by nine o'clock: and many a pleasant night they had, sitting on the sward, while the dragon told stories of old, old times, when dragons were quite plentiful and the world was a livelier place than it is now, and life was full of thrills and jumps and surprises.

What the boy had feared, however, soon came to pass. The most modest and retiring dragon in the world, if he's as big as four cart-horses and covered with blue scales, cannot be kept altogether out of the public view. And so in the village tavern of nights the fact that a real live dragon sat brooding in the cave on the Downs was naturally a subject for talk. Though the villagers were extremely frightened, they were rather proud as well. It was a distinction to have a dragon of your own, and it was felt to be a feather in the cap of the village. Still, all were agreed that this sort of thing couldn't be allowed to go on. The dreadful beast must be exterminated, the countryside must be freed from this pest, this terror, this destroying scourge. The fact that not even a hen-roost was the worse for the dragon's arrival wasn't allowed to have anything to do with it. He was a dragon, and he couldn't deny it, and if he didn't choose to behave as such that was his own look-out. But in spite of much valiant talk no hero was found willing to take sword and spear and free the suffering village and win deathless fame; and each night's heated discussion always ended in nothing. Meanwhile the dragon, a happy Bohemian, lolled on the turf, enjoyed the sunsets, told antediluvian anecdotes to the boy, and polished his old verses while meditating on fresh ones.

One day the boy, on walking into the village, found everything wearing a festal appearance which was not to be accounted for in the calendar. Carpets and gay-coloured stuffs were hung out of the windows, the church bells clamoured noisily, the little street was flower-strewn, and the whole population jostled each other along either side of it, chattering, shoving, and ordering each other to stand back. The boy saw a friend of his own age in the crowd and hailed him.

"What's up?" he cried. "Is it the players, or bears, or a circus, or what?"

"It's all right," his friend hailed back. "He's a-coming."

"*Who's* a-coming?" demanded the boy, thrusting into the throng.

"Why, St. George, of course," replied his friend. "He's heard tell of our dragon, and he's comin' on purpose to slay the deadly beast, and free us from his horrid yoke. Oh my! won't there be a jolly fight!"

Here was news indeed! The boy felt that he ought to make quite sure for himself, and he wriggled himself in between the legs of his good-natured elders, abusing them all the time for their unmannerly habit of shoving. Once in the front rank, he breathlessly awaited the arrival.

Presently from the far-away end of the line came the sound of cheering. Next, the measured tramp of a great war-horse made his heart beat quicker, and then he found himself cheering with the rest, as, amidst welcoming shouts, shrill cries of women, uplifting of babies, and waving of handkerchiefs, St. George paced slowly up the street. The boy's heart stood still and he breathed with sobs, the beauty and the grace of the hero were so far beyond anything he had yet seen. His fluted armour was inlaid with gold, his plumed helmet hung at his saddle-bow, and his thick fair hair framed a face gracious and gentle beyond expression till you caught the sternness in his eyes. He drew rein in front of the little inn, and the villagers crowded round with greetings and thanks and voluble statements of their wrongs and grievances and oppressions. The boy heard the grave gentle voice of the Saint, assuring them that all would be well now, and that he would stand by them and see them righted and free them from their foe; then he dismounted and passed through the doorway and the crowd poured in after him. But the boy made off up the hill as fast as he could lay his legs to the ground.

"It's all up, Dragon!" he shouted, as soon as he was within sight of the beast. "He's coming! He's here now! You'll have to pull yourself together and *do* something at last!"

The dragon was licking his scales and rubbing them with a bit of house-flannel the boy's mother had lent him, till he shone like a great turquoise.

"Don't be *violent,* boy," he said without looking round. "Sit down and get your breath, and try and remember that the noun governs the verb, and then perhaps you'll be good enough to tell me *who's* coming?"

"That's right, take it coolly," said the boy. "Hope you'll be half as cool when I've got through with my news. It's only St. George who's coming, that's all; he rode into the village half an hour ago. Of course you can lick him— a great big fellow like you! But I thought I'd warn you, 'cos he's sure to be round early, and he's got the longest, wickedest-looking spear you ever did see!" And the boy got up and began to jump round in sheer delight at the prospect of the battle.

"Oh deary, deary me," moaned the dragon; "this is too awful. I won't see him, and that's flat. I don't want to know the fellow at all. I'm sure he's not nice. You must tell him to go away at once, please. Say he can write if he likes, but I can't give him an interview. I'm not seeing anybody at present."

"Now, Dragon, Dragon," said the boy imploringly, "don't be perverse and wrong-headed. You've *got* to fight him some time or other, you know, 'cos he's St. George and you're the dragon. Better get it over and then we can go on with the sonnets. And you ought to consider other people a little, too. If it's been dull up here for you, think how dull it's been for me!"

"My dear little man," said the dragon solemnly, "just understand, once for all, that I can't fight and I won't fight. I've never fought in my life, and I'm not going to begin now, just to give you a Roman holiday. In old days I always let the other fellows—the *earnest* fellows—do all the fighting, and no doubt that's why I have the pleasure of being here now."

"But if you don't fight he'll cut your head off!" gasped the boy, miserable at the prospect of losing both his fight and his friend.

"Oh, I think not," said the dragon, in his lazy way. "You'll be able to arrange something. I've every confidence in you, you're such a *manager*. Just run down, there's a dear chap, and make it all right. I leave it entirely to you."

The boy made his way back to the village in a state of great despondency. First of all, there wasn't going to be any fight; next, his dear and honoured friend the dragon hadn't shown up in quite such a heroic light as he would have liked; and lastly, whether the dragon was a hero at heart or not, it made no difference, for St. George would most undoubtedly cut his head off. "Arrange things indeed!" he said bitterly to himself. "The dragon treats the whole affair as if it were an invitation to tea and croquet."

The villagers were straggling homewards as he passed up the street, all of them in the highest spirits, and gleefully discussing the splendid fight that was in store. The boy pursued his way to the inn, and passed into the principal chamber, where St. George now sat alone, musing over the chances of the fight, and the sad stories of rapine and of wrong that had so lately been poured into his sympathetic ears.

"May I come in, St. George?" said the boy politely, as he paused at the door. "I want to talk to you about this little matter of the dragon, if you're not tired of it by this time."

"Yes, come in, boy," said the Saint kindly. "Another tale of misery and wrong, I fear me. Is it a kind parent, then, of whom the tyrant has bereft you? Or some tender sister, or brother? Well, it shall soon be avenged."

"Nothing of the sort," said the boy. "There's a misunderstanding somewhere, and I want to put it right. The fact is, this is a *good* dragon."

"Exactly," said St. George, smiling pleasantly, "I quite understand. A good dragon. Believe me, I do not in the least regret that he is an adversary worthy of my steel, and no feeble specimen of his noxious tribe."

"But he's *not* a noxious tribe," cried the boy distressedly. "Oh dear, oh dear, how *stupid* men are when they get an idea into their heads! I tell you he's a *good* dragon, and a friend of mine, and tells me the most beautiful stories you ever heard, all about old times and when he was little. And he's been so kind to mother, and mother'd do anything for him. And father likes him too, though father doesn't hold with art and poetry much, and always falls asleep when the dragon starts talking about *style*. But the fact is, nobody can help liking him when once they know him. He's so engaging and so trustful, and as simple as a child!"

"Sit down, and draw your chair up," said St. George. "I like a fellow who sticks up for his friends, and I'm sure the dragon has his good points, if he's got a friend like you. But that's not the question. All this evening I've been listening, with grief and anguish unspeakable, to tales of murder, theft, and wrong; rather too highly coloured, perhaps, not always quite convincing, but forming in the main a most serious roll of crime. History teaches us that the greatest rascals often possess all the domestic virtues; and I fear that your cultivated friend, in spite of the qualities which have won (and rightly) your regard, has got to be speedily exterminated."

"Oh, you've been taking in all the yarns those fellows have been telling you," said the boy impatiently. "Why, our villagers are the biggest story-tellers in all the country round. It's a known fact. You're a stranger in these parts, or else you'd have heard it already. All they want is a *fight*. They're the most awful beggars for getting up fights—it's meat and drink to them. Dogs, bulls, dragons—anything so long as it's a fight. Why, they've got a poor innocent badger in the stable behind here, at this moment. They were going to have some fun with him to-day, but they're saving him up now till *your* little affair's over. And I've no doubt they've been telling you what a hero you were, and how you were bound to win, in the cause of right and justice, and so on; but let me tell you, I came down the street just now, and they were betting six to four on the dragon freely!"

"Six to four on the dragon!" murmured St. George sadly, resting his cheek on his hand. "This is an evil world, and sometimes I begin to think that all the wickedness in it is not entirely bottled up inside the dragons. And yet—may not this wily beast have misled you as to his real character, in order that your good report of him may serve as a cloak for his evil deeds? Nay, may there not be, at this very moment, some hapless princess immured within yonder gloomy cavern?"

The moment he had spoken, St. George was sorry for what he had said, the boy looked so genuinely distressed.

"I assure you, St. George," he said earnestly, "there's nothing of the sort in the cave at all. The dragon's a real gentleman, every inch of him, and I may say that no one would be more shocked and grieved than he would, at hearing you talk in that—that *loose* way about matters on which he has very strong views!"

"Well, perhaps I've been over-credulous," said St. George. "Perhaps I've misjudged the animal. But what are we to do? Here are the dragon and I, almost face to face, each supposed to be thirsting for each other's blood. I don't see any way out of it, exactly. What do you suggest? Can't you arrange things, somehow?"

"That's just what the dragon said," replied the boy, rather nettled. "Really, the way you two seem to leave everything to me—I suppose you couldn't be persuaded to go away quietly, could you?"

"Impossible, I fear," said the Saint. "Quite against the rules. *You* know that as well as I do."

"Well, then, look here," said the boy, "it's early yet—would you mind strolling up with me and seeing the dragon and talking it over? It's not far, and any friend of mine will be most welcome."

"Well, it's *irregular*," said St. George, rising, "but really it seems about the most sensible thing to do. You're taking a lot of trouble on your friend's account," he added good-naturedly, as they passed out through the door together. "But cheer up! Perhaps there won't have to be any fight after all."

"Oh, but I hope there will, though!" replied the little fellow wistfully.

"I've brought a friend to see you, Dragon," said the boy rather loud.

The dragon woke up with a start. "I was just—er—thinking about things," he said in his simple way. "Very pleased to make your acquaintance, sir. Charming weather we're having!"

"This is St. George," said the boy shortly. "St. George, let me introduce you to the dragon. We've come up to talk things over quietly, Dragon, and now for goodness' sake do let us have a little straight common sense, and come to some practical business-like arrangement, for I'm sick of views and theories of life and personal tendencies, and all that sort of thing. I may perhaps add that my mother's sitting up."

"So glad to meet you, St. George," began the dragon rather nervously, "because you've been a great traveller, I hear, and I've always been rather a stay-at-home. But I can show you many antiquities, many interesting features of our countryside, if you're stopping here any time—"

"I think," said St. George, in his frank, pleasant way, "that we'd really better take the advice of our young friend here, and try to come to some understanding, on a

95

business footing, about this little affair of ours. Now don't you think that after all the simplest plan would be just to fight it out, according to the rules, and let the best man win? They're betting on you, I tell you, down in the village, but I don't mind that!"

"Oh yes, *do,* Dragon," said the boy delightedly; "it'll save such a lot of bother!"

"My young friend, you shut up," said the dragon severely. "Believe me, St. George," he went on, "there's nobody in the world I'd sooner oblige than you and this young gentleman here. But the whole thing's nonsense, and conventionality, and popular thick-headedness. There's absolutely nothing to fight about, from beginning to end. And anyhow I'm not going to, so that settles it!"

"But supposing I make you?" said St. George, rather nettled.

"You can't," said the dragon triumphantly. "I should only go into my cave and retire for a time down the hole I came up. You'd soon get heartily sick of sitting outside and waiting for me to come out and fight you. And as soon as you'd really gone away, why, I'd come up again gaily, for I tell you frankly, I like this place, and I'm going to stay here!"

St. George gazed for a while on the fair landscape around them. "But this would be a beautiful place for a fight," he began again persuasively. "These great bare rolling Downs for the arena—and me in my golden armour showing up against your big, blue, scaly coils! Think what a picture it would make!"

"Now you're trying to get at me through my artistic sensibilities," said the dragon. "But it won't work. Not but what it would make a very pretty picture, as you say," he added, wavering a little.

"We seem to be getting rather nearer to *business,*" put in the boy. "You must see, Dragon, that there's got to be a fight of some sort, 'cos you can't want to have to go down that dirty old hole again and stop there till goodness knows when."

"It might be arranged," said St. George thoughtfully. "I *must* spear you somewhere, of course, but I'm not bound to hurt you very much. There's such a lot of you that there must be a few *spare* places somewhere. Here, for instance, just behind your foreleg. It couldn't hurt you much, just here!"

"Now you're tickling, George," said the dragon coyly. "No, that place won't do at all. Even if it didn't hurt—and I'm sure it would, awfully—it would make me laugh, and that would spoil everything."

"Let's try somewhere else, then," said St. George patiently. "Under your neck, for instance—all these folds of thick skin—if I speared you here you'd never even know I'd done it!"

"Yes, but are you sure you can hit off the right place?" asked the dragon anxiously.

"Of course I am," said St. George, with confidence. "You leave that to me!"

"It's just because I've *got* to leave it to you that I'm asking," replied the dragon rather testily. "No doubt you would deeply regret any error you might make in the hurry of the moment; but you wouldn't regret it half as much as I should! However, I suppose we've got to trust somebody, as we go through life, and your plan seems, on the whole, as good a one as any."

"Look here, dragon," interrupted the boy, a little jealous on behalf of his friend, who seemed to be getting all the worst of the bargain, "I don't quite see where *you* come in! There's to be a fight, apparently, and you're to be licked; and what I want to know is, what are *you* going to get out of it?"

"St. George," said the dragon, "just tell him, please—

what will happen after I'm vanquished in the deadly combat?"

"Well, according to the rules I suppose I shall lead you in triumph down to the market-place or whatever answers to it," said St. George.

"Precisely," said the dragon. "And then—?"

"And then there'll be shoutings and speeches and things," continued St. George. "And I shall explain that you're converted, and see the error of your ways, and so on."

"Quite so," said the dragon. "And then?"

"Oh, and then—" said St. George; "why, and then there will be the usual banquet, I suppose."

"Exactly," said the dragon; "and that's where *I* come in. Look here," he continued, addressing the boy, "I'm bored to death up here, and no one really appreciates me. I'm going into Society, I am, through the kindly aid of our friend here, who's taking such a lot of trouble on my account; and you'll find I've got all the qualities to endear me to people who entertain! So now that's all settled, and if you don't mind—I'm an old-fashioned fellow—don't want to turn you out, but—"

"Remember, you'll have to do your proper share of the fighting, Dragon!" said St. George, as he took the hint and rose to go; "I mean ramping, and breathing fire, and so on!"

"I can *ramp* all right," replied the dragon confidently; "as to breathing fire, it's surprising how easily one gets out of practice; but I'll do the best I can. Good night!"

They had descended the hill and were almost back in the village again, when St. George stopped short. "*Knew* I had forgotten something," he said. "There ought to be a princess. Terror-stricken and chained to a rock, and all that sort of thing. Boy, can't you arrange a princess?"

The boy was in the middle of a tremendous yawn. "I'm tired to death," he wailed, "and I *can't* arrange a princess, or anything more, at this time of night. And my mother's sitting up, and *do* stop asking me to arrange more things till to-morrow!"

Next morning the people began streaming up to the Downs at quite an early hour, in their Sunday clothes and carrying baskets with bottle-necks sticking out of them, everyone intent on securing good places for the combat. This was not exactly a simple matter, for of course it was quite possible that the dragon might win, and in that case even those who had put their money on him felt they could hardly expect him to deal with his backers on a different footing to the rest. Places were chosen, therefore, with circumspection and with a view to a speedy retreat in case of emergency; and the front rank was mostly composed of boys who had escaped from parental control and now sprawled and rolled about on the grass, regardless of the shrill threats and warnings discharged at them by their anxious mothers behind.

The boy had secured a good front place, well up towards the cave, and was feeling as anxious as a stage-manager on a first night. Could the dragon be depended upon? He might change his mind and vote the whole performance rot; or else, seeing that the affair had been so hastily planned without even a rehearsal, he might be too nervous to show up. The boy looked narrowly at the cave, but it showed no sign of life or occupation. Could the dragon have made a moonlight flitting?

The higher portions of the ground were now black with sight-seers, and presently a sound of cheering and a waving of handkerchiefs told that something was visible to them which the boy, far up towards the dragon-end of the line as he was, could not yet see. A minute more and

St. George's red plumes topped the hill, as the Saint rode slowly forth on the great level space which stretched up to the grim mouth of the cave. Very gallant and beautiful he looked on his tall war-horse, his golden armour glancing in the sun, his great spear held erect, the little white pennon, crimson-crossed, fluttering at its point. He drew rein and remained motionless. The lines of spectators began to give back a little nervously; and even the boys in front stopped pulling hair and cuffing each other, and leaned forward expectant.

"Now then, Dragon!" muttered the boy impatiently, fidgeting where he sat. He need not have distressed himself, had he only known. The dramatic possibilities of the thing had tickled the dragon immensely, and he had been up from an early hour, preparing for his first public appearance with as much heartiness as if the years had run backwards, and he had been again a little dragonlet, playing with his sisters on the floor of their mother's cave, at the game of saints-and-dragons, in which the dragon was bound to win.

A low muttering, mingled with snorts, now made itself heard; rising to a bellowing roar that seemed to fill the plain. Then a cloud of smoke obscured the mouth of the cave, and out of the midst of it the dragon himself, shining, sea-blue, magnificent, pranced splendidly forth; and everybody said, "Oo-oo-oo!" as if he had been a mighty rocket! His scales were glittering, his long spiky tail lashed his sides, his claws tore up the turf and sent it flying high over his back, and smoke and fire incessantly jetted from his angry nostrils. "Oh, well done, Dragon!" cried the boy excitedly. "Didn't think he had it in him!" he added to himself.

St. George lowered his spear, bent his head, dug his heels into his horse's sides, and came thundering over the turf. The dragon charged with a roar and a squeal—

a great, blue, whirling combination of coils and snorts and clashing jaws and spikes and fire.

"Missed!" yelled the crowd. There was a moment's entanglement of golden armour and blue-green coils and spiky tail, and then the great horse, tearing at his bit, carried the Saint, his spear swung high in the air, almost up to the mouth of the cave.

The dragon sat down and barked viciously, while St. George with difficulty pulled his horse round into position.

"End of Round One!" thought the boy. "How well they managed it! But I hope the Saint won't get excited. I can trust the dragon all right. What a regular play-actor the fellow is!"

St. George had at last prevailed on his horse to stand steady, and was looking round him as he wiped his brow. Catching sight of the boy, he smiled and nodded, and held up three fingers for an instant.

"It seems to be all planned out," said the boy to himself. "Round Three is to be the finishing one, evidently. Wish it could have lasted a bit longer. Whatever's that old fool of a dragon up to now?"

The dragon was employing the interval in giving a ramping performance for the benefit of the crowd. Ramping, it should be explained, consists in running round and round in a wide circle, and sending waves and ripples of movement along the whole length of your spine, from your pointed ears right down to the spike at the end of your long tail. When you are covered with blue scales, the effect is particularly pleasing; and the boy recollected the dragon's recently expressed wish to become a social success.

St. George now gathered up his reins and began to move forward, dropping the point of his spear and settling himself firmly in the saddle.

"Time!" yelled everybody excitedly; and the dragon, leaving off his ramping, sat up on end, and began to leap from one side to the other with huge ungainly bounds, whooping like a Red Indian. This naturally disconcerted the horse, who swerved violently, the Saint only just saving himself by the mane; and as they shot past the dragon delivered a vicious snap at the horse's tail which sent the poor beast careening madly far over the Downs, so that the language of the Saint, who had lost a stirrup, was fortunately inaudible to the general assemblage.

Round Two evoked audible evidence of friendly feeling towards the dragon. The spectators were not slow to appreciate a combatant who could hold his own so well and clearly wanted to show good sport; and many encouraging remarks reached the ears of our friend as he strutted to and fro, his chest thrust out and his tail in the air, hugely enjoying his new popularity.

St. George had dismounted and was tightening his girths, and telling his horse, with quite an oriental flow of imagery, exactly what he thought of him, and his relations, and his conduct on the present occasion; so the boy made his way down to the Saint's end of the line, and held his spear for him.

"It's been a jolly fight, St. George!" he said with a sigh. "Can't you let it last a bit longer?"

"Well, I think I'd better not," replied the Saint. "The fact is, your simple-minded old friend's getting conceited, now they've begun cheering him, and he'll forget all about the arrangement and take to playing the fool, and there's no telling where he would stop. I'll just finish him off this round."

He swung himself into the saddle and took his spear from the boy. "Now don't you be afraid," he added kindly. "I've marked my spot exactly, and *he's* sure to give me all the assistance in his power, because he knows it's his only chance of being asked to the banquet!"

St. George now shortened his spear, bringing the butt well up under his arm; and, instead of galloping as before, trotted smartly towards the dragon, who crouched at his approach, flicking his tail till it cracked in the air like a great cart-whip. The Saint wheeled as he neared his opponent and circled warily round him, keeping his eye on the spare place; while the dragon, adopting similar tactics, paced with caution round the same circle, occasionally feinting with his head. So the two sparred for an opening, while the spectators maintained a breathless silence.

Though the round lasted for some minutes, the end was so swift that all the boy saw was a lightning movement of the Saint's arm, and then a whirl and a confusion of spines, claws, tail, and flying bits of turf. The dust cleared away, the spectators whooped and ran in cheering, and the boy made out that the dragon was down, pinned to the earth by the spear, while St. George had dismounted, and stood astride of him.

It all seemed so genuine that the boy ran in breathlessly, hoping the dear old dragon wasn't really hurt. As he approached, the dragon lifted one large eyelid, winked solemnly, and collapsed again. He was held fast to earth by the neck, but the Saint had hit him in the spare place agreed upon, and it didn't even seem to tickle.

"Bain't you goin' to cut 'is 'ed orf, master!" asked one of the applauding crowd. He had backed the dragon, and naturally felt a trifle sore.

"Well, not *to-day*, I think," replied St. George pleasantly. "You see, that can be done at *any* time. There's no hurry at all. I think we'll all go down to the village first, and have some refreshment, and then I'll give him a good talking-to, and you'll find he'll be a very different dragon!"

At that magic word *refreshment* the whole crowd awaited the signal to start. The time for talking and cheering and betting was past, the hour for action had arrived. St. George, hauling on his spear with both hands, released the dragon, who rose and shook himself and ran his eye over his spikes and scales and things, to see that they were all in order. Then the Saint mounted and led off the procession, the dragon following meekly in the company of the boy, while the thirsty spectators kept at a respectful interval behind.

There were great doings when they got down to the village again, and had formed up in front of the inn. After refreshment St. George made a speech, in which he informed his audience that he had removed their direful scourge, at a great deal of trouble and inconvenience to himself, and now they weren't to go about grumbling and fancying they'd got grievances, because they hadn't. And they shouldn't be so fond of fights, because next time they might have to do the fighting themselves, which would not be the same thing at all. And there was a certain badger in the inn stables which had got to be released at once, and he'd come and see it done himself. Then he told them that the dragon had been thinking over things, and saw that there were two sides to every question, and he wasn't going to do it any more, and if they were good perhaps he'd stay and settle down there. So they must make friends, and not be prejudiced, and go about fancying they knew everything there was to be known, because they didn't, not by a long way. And he warned them against the sin of romancing, and making up stories and fancying other people would believe them just because they were plausible and highly coloured. Then he sat down, amidst much repentant cheering, and the dragon nudged the boy in the ribs and whispered that

104

he couldn't have done it better himself. Then everyone went off to get ready for the banquet.

Banquets are always pleasant things, consisting mostly, as they do, of eating and drinking; but the specially nice thing about a banquet is, that it comes when something's over, and there's nothing more to worry about, and to-morrow seems a long way off. St. George was happy because there had been a fight and he hadn't had to kill anybody; for he didn't really like killing, though he generally had to do it. The dragon was happy because there had been a fight, and so far from being hurt in it he had won popularity and a sure footing in society. The boy was happy because there had been a fight, and in spite of it all his two friends were on the best of terms. And all the others were happy because there had been a fight, and—well, they didn't require any other reasons for their happiness. The dragon exerted himself to say the right thing to everybody, and proved the life and soul of the evening; while the Saint and the boy, as they looked on, felt that they were only assisting at a feast of which the honour and the glory were entirely the dragon's. But they didn't mind that, being good fellows, and the dragon was not in the least proud or forgetful. On the contrary, every ten minutes or so he leant over towards the boy and said impressively; "Look here! you *will* see me home afterwards, won't you!" And the boy always nodded, though he had promised his mother not to be out late.

At last the banquet was over, the guests had dropped away with many good nights and congratulations and invitations, and the dragon, who had seen the last of them off the premises, emerged into the street followed by the boy, wiped his brow, sighed, sat down in the road and gazed at the stars. "Jolly night it's been!" he murmured. "Jolly stars! Jolly little place this! Think I shall just stop here. Don't feel like climbing up any beastly hill. Boy's promised to see me home. Boy had better do it then! No responsibility on my part. Responsibility all boy's!" And his chin sank on his broad chest and he slumbered peacefully.

"Oh, *get* up, Dragon," cried the boy piteously. "You *know* my mother's sitting up, and I'm so tired, and you made me promise to see you home, and I never knew what it meant or I wouldn't have done it!" And the boy sat down in the road by the side of the sleeping dragon and cried.

The door behind them opened, a stream of light illumined the road, and St. George, who had come out for a stroll in the cool night air, caught sight of the two figures sitting there—the great motionless dragon and the tearful little boy.

"What's the matter, boy?" he inquired kindly, stepping to his side.

"Oh, it's this great lumbering *pig* of a dragon!" sobbed the boy. "First he makes me promise to see him home, and then he says I'd better do it, and goes to sleep! Might as well try to see a *haystack* home! And I'm so tired, and mother's—" Here he broke down again.

"Now don't take on," said St. George. "I'll stand by you, and we'll *both* see him home. Wake up, dragon!" he said sharply, shaking the beast by the elbow.

The dragon looked up sleepily. "What a night, George!" he murmured; "what a—"

"Now look here, Dragon," said the Saint firmly. "Here's this little fellow waiting to see you home, and you *know* he ought to have been in bed these two hours, and what his mother'll say *I* don't know, and anybody but a selfish pig would have *made* him go to bed long ago—"

"And he *shall* go to bed!" cried the dragon, starting

up. "Poor little chap, only fancy his being up at this hour! It's a shame, that's what it is, and I don't think, St. George, you've been very considerate—but come along at once, and don't let us have any more arguing or shilly-shallying. You give me hold of your hand, boy—thank you, George, an arm up the hill is just what I wanted!"

So they set off up the hill arm-in-arm, the Saint, the dragon, and the boy. The lights in the little village began to go out; but there were stars, and a late moon, as they climbed to the Downs together. And, as they turned the last corner and disappeared from view, snatches of an old song were borne back on the night breeze. I can't be certain which of them was singing, but I *think* it was the dragon!

IV · THE UNICORN

The lore of the unicorn is more extensive than that of any other of the mythical beasts. The historians of the Renaissance devoted much time to discussing this curious animal, and during the whole of the Middle Ages it was surrounded by miraculous legends, many of which derived from remote antiquity.

The first written account of the unicorn was given by Ctesias, a Greek historian who visited the court of the King of Persia in the fourth century B.C.

Ctesias

FROM CERTAIN WILD ASSES

There are in India certain wild asses which are as large as horses or larger. Their bodies are white, their heads dark red, and their eyes dark blue. They have a horn on the forehead which is about a foot and a half in length. . . . The dust filed from the horn is administered in a potion as a protection against deadly poisons.

Pliny, the Roman naturalist, took up the story in the first century A.D. and expanded upon it, and by the fourth century tales of unicorns were quite common. It was about this time that the story of the unicorn hunt first appeared. The unicorn was described as a fierce animal, impossible to capture except through treachery by a beautiful maiden. This maiden had to go sit at the foot of a tree deep in the forest and wait for the unicorn to appear. Attracted by her beauty, the animal would come and meekly lay its head in her lap. Then the hunters would come out of hiding with their spears and surround it. Bartholomaeus Anglicus, a thirteenth-century English monk, tells us about the unicorn in his compendium of universal knowledge, *De Proprietatibus Rerum*.

Bartholomaeus Anglicus

ON THE NATURE OF UNICORNS

An Unicorn is a right cruel beast, and hath that name for he hath in the middle of the forehead an horn of four foot long; and that horn is so sharp and so strong, that he is not taken with might of hunters; but a maid is set there as he shall come, and she openeth her lap, and the Unicorn layeth thereon his head, and leaveth all his fierceness, and sleepeth in that wise, and is taken as a beast without weapon, and slain with darts of hunters. The Unicorn froteth [rubs] and fileth his horn against stones, and sharpeth it, and maketh it ready to fight in that wise. And his colour is bay. There be many kinds of Unicorns, for some be Rhinoceros (q.v.), and some *Monoceron,* and *Aegloceron.* And *Monoceron* is a wild beast, shaped like to the horse in body, and to the hart in head, and in the feet to the elephant, and in the tail to the boar, and hath heavy lowing, and an horn strutting in the middle of the forehead of two cubits long. And in Ind be some one-horned asses, and such an ass is called *Monoceros,* and is less bold and fierce than other Unicorns.

By the Middle Ages the unicorn had made a secure place for itself in European folklore. There was no reason to doubt its existence, for it did not look very different from a horse or a deer, except for the single horn in the middle of its forehead. Here it is described by Lewis Varthema, a contemporary of Magellan, who was the first European to go to the sacred Moslem city of Mecca with a pilgrim caravan through the Arabian Desert (his travels took place between 1502 and 1508) and to write an account of his pilgrimage:

Lewis Varthema

UNICORNS IN MECCA

On the other part of the Temple are Parkes or places inclosed, where are seene two Unicornes, and are there shewed to the people for a wonder. The one of them, which is much higher than the other, yet not much unlike to a Colt of thirtie monthes of age; in the fore-head groweth only one Horne, in manner right forth, of the length of three Cubits. The other is much younger, and like a young Colt: of the age of one yeare; the horne of this, is of the length of foure spannes. This beast is of the colour of a Horse of Weesell colour, and hath the head like an Hart, but no long necke, a thinne mane hanging only on the one side: their legs are thinne and slender, like a Fawne or Hind: the hoofes of the fore-feet are divided in two, much like the feet of a Goat, the outward part of the hinder feet is very full of haire. This beast doubtlesse seemeth wild and fierce, yet tempereth that fiercenesse with a certaine comelinesse. These Unicornes one gave to the Sultan of Mecca, as a most precious and rare gift. They were sent him out of Ethiopia by a King of that Countrey, who desired by that present to gratifie the Sultan of Mecca.

There are many myths concerning the magic powers of the unicorn's horn, going right back to Ctesias. From earliest times physicians and scholars believed that powdered horn was a cure for almost every disease, as well as a sure protection against poison. Thus fragments of horn were very valuable, and an entire horn, it was said, was worth a city.

Unicorn lore has remained with us into modern times, though we now know that the unicorn could never have existed. Research has proved that no animal with cloven hoofs could ever have a single horn in the middle of his forehead, because of the way the bones must grow together before the animal is born.

Here are two modern treatments of the unicorn myth. The first is a short fantasy by Herb Lehrman, describing the meeting between a unicorn and a univac who have been put out to pasture together. The second is a powerful story of love and hate, of good and evil, told by that master storyteller of science fiction and fantasy Theodore Sturgeon.

Herb Lehrman

THE ANCIENT LAST

He was the last of his line and they put him out to pasture in an emerald field where the youngers, streamlined and genetically sleek, could come to watch and know what real power was. It was there all right, muscles rippling beneath massive shoulders. And that solid, proud, Oh! so-proud, head with the twisted horn that reached for the sky; scarred, cracked with age, blunted by time and battle, it was still a thing of magic in a universe of wonder.

He cantered there on the green, the last of the great Unicorns, and ran across the turf to show there was still spring in his legs and power in that deep milky chest. And tiring on occasion, with the weariness immortals sometimes feel, he would sit and remember the maidens, the wishes fulfilled in an age when his name was a clarion of virility.

Near the ancient fields of his universe, a little to the right of where he slept, the young bucks, stalwarts all, during the blackness of one long night left a thing to mock him. It was a machine, rusted and broken, its circuits no longer what they had been. A castaway from the universe of man, which somehow had come into this world of magic to lie in the center of the field. It was a cruel snub, a reminder he too was old and like the machine near useless.

"What are you?" asked the ancient greybeard, overcome with the curiosity that had borne him through the ages. "Who are you to defile my sanctuary?"

"Yak, yak, that's a busted Univac." The young bucks sneered in unison, thumbing their golden horn-nubs at the old one's stupidity.

He tossed his head and made as if to rush them. His rheumy old eyes flashed fire and that grey blunt horn lowered, whistling in the cold blue air. And they ran before the power, the force still there.

He turned then, cantering proudly back to the machine. "I too know what it means to be discarded. Cast away! . . . I'll show them there's stuff still left in both of us."

And having known all the knowledge of man, having bent his shoulders before millennia of wishes, the old Unicorn set to, to make the Univac whole again.

He labored day. He labored night, changing a wire here, weaving a gold strand there, commanding a crystal to warp, a relay to snap. But for all his craft and work and sweat—no matter how he made it gleam and hiss—the fact was plain. The Univac was a dolt, a lesser thing of logic which could not conceive of beauty.

"The trouble is, you have no heart," the old Unicorn said one day, tiring of asking his new friend questions to which he already knew the answers. "You have no juice, no loins to feel the power of life."

"There is beauty in the perfection of logic, in an equation with balance, in a question answered," replied the machine, using his new gift of speech laboriously. "Of this other thing, of this I know nothing, being only a machine."

"Live then," the old one said, making his voice magic. "Live then and know what means the slow cloud a man can bring to a woman's eye, the feel of rain, the thrill of battles won."

Alas, no magic, no spell could breach the ranks of solid-state devices, and the machine stood mutely, devoid of desire. "What is it you wish?" it said finally. "What do you want of me? A memory? A dream? I have the first but the second lives in a different realm, forever hidden, denied to me."

"Ah, it is a sad thing then. For memory is not enough. It's the dream which counts. The dream that one is still young, still beautiful, still filled with life."

"It must be wonderful," said Univac. "I wish I could dream with you, my dearest friend." And with a sudden surge of never-before-felt current its circuits all overloaded and it melted into a pile of slag.

The oldest Unicorn first grew *old* then; his horn became heavy, his neck bowed, and the youngers no longer came to mock him. Instead they came to revere him, to pay homage to his cracked voice, his senile wisdom.

Finally one day as the old one lay warming his sore withers in the sun the strongest of the young came upon him. "Old one," he said, "tell me, did the machine die of stupidity?"

"No," was the answer. "It died of something only the very old, the very discarded, die of. The very thing which will some day claim you and claim me when even I grow too old to bear the pain and the burden of my memories."

"What is that?" said the younger.

"You gambol with the maidens and give it a name," said the old one. "But what I call by that name is something else again."

And, seeing the brightness burning in the younger, feeling the budding vigor and strong life, he knew he too must finally give way.

The smaller golden beast sat silent. He knew truth when he faced it, and there in the twilight of an emerald field he came to manhood, wiser than most. So wise, indeed, he did not need to hear the old one's final, almost bitter words. "Like I, it died of love."

115

Theodore Sturgeon

THE SILKEN-SWIFT . . .

There's a village by the Bogs, and in the village is a Great House. In the Great House lived a squire who had land and treasures and, for a daughter, Rita.

In the village lived Del, whose voice was a thunder in the inn where he drank there; whose corded, cabled body was golden-skinned, and whose hair flung challenges back to the sun.

Deep in the Bogs, which were brackish, there was a pool of purest water, shaded by willows and wide-wondering aspens, cupped by banks of a moss most marvellously blue. Here grew mandrake, and there were strange pipings in midsummer. No one ever heard them but a quiet girl whose beauty was so very contained that none of it showed. Her name was Barbara.

There was a green evening, breathless with growth, when Del took his usual way down the lane beside the manor and saw a white shadow adrift inside the tall iron pickets. He stopped, and the shadow approached, and became Rita. "Slip around to the gate," she said, "and I'll open it for you."

She wore a gown like a cloud and a silver circlet round her head. Night was caught in her hair, moonlight in her face, and in her great eyes, secrets swam.

Del said, "I have no business with the squire."

"He's gone," she said. "I've sent the servants away. Come to the gate."

"I need no gate." He leaped and caught the top bar of the fence, and in a continuous fluid motion went high and across and down beside her. She looked at his arms, one, the other; then up at his hair. She pressed her small hands tight together and made a little laugh, and then she was gone through the tailored trees, lightly, swiftly, not looking back. He followed, one step for three of hers, keeping pace with a new pounding in the sides of his neck. They crossed a flower bed and a wide marble terrace. There was an open door, and when he passed through it he stopped, for she was nowhere in sight. Then the door clicked shut behind him and he whirled. She was there, her back to the panel, laughing up at him in the dimness. He thought she would come to him then, but instead she twisted by, close, her eyes on his. She smelt of violets and sandalwood. He followed her into a great hall, quite dark but full of the subdued lights of polished wood, cloisonné, tooled leather and gold-threaded tapestry. She flung open another door, and they were in a small room with a carpet made of rosy silences, and a candle-lit table. Two places were set, each with five different crystal glasses and old silver as prodigally used as the iron pickets outside. Six teakwood steps rose to a great oval window. "The moon," she said, "will rise for us there."

She motioned him to a chair and crossed to a sideboard, where there was a rack of decanters—ruby wine and white; one with a strange brown bead; pink and amber. She took down the first and poured. Then she lifted the silver domes from the salvers on the table, and a magic of fragrance filled the air. There were smoking sweets and savories, rare seafood and slivers of fowl, and morsels of strange meat wrapped in flower petals, spitted with foreign fruits and tiny soft seashells. All about were spices, each like a separate voice in the distant murmur of a crowd: saffron and sesame, cumin and marjoram and mace.

And all the while Del watched her in wonder, seeing how the candles left the moonlight in her face, and how completely she trusted her hands, which did such deftness without supervision—so composed she was, for all the silent secret laughter that tugged at her lips, for all the bright dark mysteries that swirled and swam within her.

They ate, and the oval window yellowed and darkened while the candlelight grew bright. She poured another wine, and another, and with the courses of the meal they were as May to the crocus and as frost to the apple.

Del knew it was alchemy and he yielded to it without question. That which was purposely over-sweet would be piquantly cut; this induced thirst would, with exquisite timing, be quenched. He knew she was watching him; he knew she was aware of the heat in his cheeks and the tingle at his fingertips. His wonder grew, but he was not afraid.

In all this time she spoke hardly a word; but at last the feast was over and they rose. She touched a silken rope on the wall, and panelling slid aside. The table rolled silently into some ingenious recess and the panel returned. She waved him to an L-shaped couch in one corner, and as he sat close to her, she turned and took down the lute which hung on the wall behind her. He had his moment of confusion; his arms were ready for her, but not for the instrument as well. Her eyes sparkled, but her composure was unshaken.

Now she spoke, while her fingers strolled and danced on the lute, and her words marched and wandered in and about the music. She had a thousand voices, so that he wondered which of them was truly hers. Sometimes she sang; sometimes it was a wordless crooning. She seemed at times remote from him, puzzled at the turn the music was taking, and at other times she seemed to hear the pulsing roar in his eardrums, and she played laughing syncopations to it. She sang words which he almost understood:

> *Bee to blossom, honey dew,*
> *Claw to mouse, and rain to tree,*
> *Moon to midnight, I to you;*
> *Sun to starlight, you to me . . .*

and she sang something wordless:

> *Ake ya rundefle, rundefle fye,*
> *Orel ya rundefle kown,*
> *En yea, en yea, ya bunderbee bye*
> *En sor, en see, en sown.*

which he also almost understood.

In still another voice she told him the story of a great hairy spider and a little pink girl who found it between the leaves of a half-open book; and at first he was all fright and pity for the girl, but then she went on to tell of what the spider suffered, with his home disrupted by this yawping giant, and so vividly did she tell of it that at the end he was laughing at himself and all but crying for the poor spider.

So the hours slipped by, and suddenly, between songs, she was in his arms; and in the instant she had twisted up and away from him, leaving him gasping. She said, in still a new voice, sober and low, "No, Del. We must wait for the moon."

His thighs ached and he realized that he had half-risen, arms out, hands clutching and feeling the extraordinary fabric of her gown, though it was gone from them; and he sank back to the couch with an odd, faint sound that was wrong for the room. He flexed his fingers and, reluctantly, the sensation of white gossamer left them. At last he looked across at her and she laughed and leapt high lightly, and it was as if she stopped in midair to stretch for a moment before she alighted beside him, bent and kissed his mouth, and leapt away.

The roaring in his ears was greater, and at this it

seemed to acquire a tangible weight. His head bowed; he tucked his knuckles into the upper curve of his eye sockets and rested his elbows on his knees. He could hear the sweet sussurrus of Rita's gown as she moved about the room; he could sense the violets and sandalwood. She was dancing, immersed in the joy of movement and of his nearness. She made her own music, humming, sometimes whispering to the melodies in her mind.

And at length he became aware that she had stopped; he could hear nothing, though he knew she was still near. Heavily he raised his head. She was in the center of the room, balanced like a huge white moth, her eyes quite dark now with their secrets quiet. She was staring at the window, poised, waiting.

He followed her gaze. The big oval was black no longer, but dusted over with silver light. Del rose slowly. The dust was a mist, a loom, and then, at one edge, there was a shard of the moon itself creeping and growing.

Because Del stopped breathing, he could hear her breathe; it was rapid and so deep it faintly strummed her versatile vocal cords.

"Rita . . ."

Without answering she ran to the sideboard and filled two small glasses. She gave him one, then, "Wait," she breathed, "oh, wait!"

Spellbound, he waited while the white stain crept across the window. He understood suddenly that he must be still until the great oval was completely filled with direct moonlight, and this helped him, because it set a foreseeable limit to his waiting; and it hurt him, because nothing in life, he thought, had ever moved so slowly. He had a moment of rebellion, in which he damned himself for falling in with her complex pacing; but with it he realized that now the darker silver was wasting away, now it was a finger's breadth, and now a thread, and now, and *now*—.

She made a brittle feline cry and sprang up the dark steps to the window. So bright was the light that her body was a jet cameo against it. So delicately wrought was her gown that he could see the epaulettes of silver light the moon gave her. She was so beautiful his eyes stung.

"Drink," she whispered. "Drink with me, darling, darling. . . ."

For an instant he did not understand her at all, and only gradually did he become aware of the little glass he held. He raised it toward her and drank. And of all the twists and titillations of taste he had had this night, this was the most startling; for it had no taste at all, almost no substance, and a temperature almost exactly that of blood. He looked stupidly down at the glass and back up at the girl. He thought that she had turned about and was watching him, though he could not be sure, since her silhouette was the same.

And then he had his second of unbearable shock, for the light went out.

The moon was gone, the window, the room, Rita was gone.

For a stunned instant he stood tautly, stretching his eyes wide. He made a sound that was not a word. He dropped the glass and pressed his palms to his eyes, feeling them blink, feeling the stiff silk of his lashes against them. Then he snatched the hands away, and it was still dark, and more than dark; this was not a blackness. This was like trying to see with an elbow or with a tongue; it was not black, it was *Nothingness.*

He fell to his knees.

Rita laughed.

An odd, alert part of his mind seized on the laugh

and understood it, and horror and fury spread through his whole being; for this was the laugh which had been tugging at her lips all evening, and it was a hard, cruel, self-assured laugh. And at the same time, because of the anger or in spite of it, desire exploded whitely within him. He moved toward the sound, groping, mouthing. There was a quick, faint series of rustling sounds from the steps, and then a light, strong web fell around him. He struck out at it, and recognized it for the unforgettable thing it was—her robe. He caught at it, ripped it, stamped upon it. He heard her bare feet run lightly down and past him, and lunged, and caught nothing. He stood, gasping painfully.

She laughed again.

"I'm blind," he said hoarsely. "Rita, I'm blind!"

"I know," she said coolly, close beside him. And again she laughed.

"What have you done to me?"

"I've watched you be a dirty animal of a man," she said.

He grunted and lunged again. His knees struck something—a chair, a cabinet—and he fell heavily. He thought he touched her foot.

"Here, lover, here!" she taunted.

He fumbled about for the thing which had tripped him, found it, used it to help him upright again. He peered uselessly about.

"Here, lover!"

He leaped, and crashed into the door jamb: cheekbone, collarbone, hipbone, ankle were one straight blaze of pain. He clung to the polished wood.

After a time he said, in agony, "Why?"

"No man has ever touched me and none ever will," she sang. Her breath was on his cheek. He reached and touched nothing, and then he heard her leap from her perch on a statue's pedestal by the door, where she had stood high and leaned over to speak.

No pain, no blindness, not even the understanding that it was her witch's brew working in him could quell the wild desire he felt at her nearness. Nothing could tame the fury that shook him as she laughed. He staggered after her, bellowing.

She danced around him, laughing. Once she pushed him into a clattering rack of fire irons. Once she caught his elbow from behind and spun him. And once, incredibly, she sprang past him and, in midair, kissed him again on the mouth.

He descended into Hell, surrounded by the small, sure patter of bare feet and sweet cool laughter. He rushed and crashed, he crouched and bled and whimpered like a hound. His roaring and blundering took an echo, and that must have been the great hall. Then there were walls that seemed more than unyielding; they struck back. And there were panels to lean against, gasping, which became opening doors as he leaned. And always the black nothingness, the writhing temptation of the pat-pat of firm flesh on smooth stones, and the ravening fury.

It was cooler, and there was no echo. He became aware of the whisper of the wind through trees. The balcony, he thought; and then, right in his ear, so that he felt her warm breath, "Come, lover. . . ." and he sprang. He sprang and missed, and instead of sprawling on the terrace, there was nothing, and nothing, and nothing, and then, when he least expected it, a shower of cruel thumps as he rolled down the marble steps.

He must have had a shred of consciousness left, for he was vaguely aware of the approach of her bare feet, and of the small, cautious hand that touched his shoulder and moved to his mouth, and then his chest. Then it was withdrawn, and either she laughed or the sound was still in his mind.

Deep in the Bogs, which were brackish, there was a pool of purest water, shaded by willows and wide-wondering aspens, cupped by banks of a moss most marvellously blue. Here grew mandrake, and there were strange pipings in midsummer. No one ever heard them but a quiet girl whose beauty was so very contained that none of it showed. Her name was Barbara.

No one noticed Barbara, no one lived with her, no one cared. And Barbara's life was very full, for she was born to receive. Others are born wishing to receive, so they wear bright masks and make attractive sounds like cicadas and operettas, so others will be forced, one way or another, to give to them. But Barbara's receptors were wide open, and always had been, so that she needed no substitute for sunlight through a tulip petal, or the sound of morning-glories climbing, or the tangy sweet smell of formic acid which is the only death cry possible to an ant, or any other of the thousand things overlooked by folk who can only wish to receive. Barbara had a garden and an orchard, and took things in to market when she cared to, and the rest of the time she spent in taking what was given. Weeds grew in her garden, but since they were welcomed, they grew only where they could keep the watermelons from being sunburned. The rabbits were welcome, so they kept to the two rows of carrots, the one of lettuce, and the one of tomato vines which were planted for them, and they left the rest alone. Goldenrod shot up beside the bean hills to lend a hand upward, and the birds ate only the figs and peaches from the waviest top branches, and in return patrolled the lower ones for caterpillars and egg-laying flies. And if a fruit stayed green for two weeks longer until Barbara had time to go to market, or if a mole could channel moisture to the roots of the corn, why it was the least they could do.

For a brace of years Barbara had wandered more and more, impelled by a thing she could not name—if indeed she was aware of it at all. She knew only that over-the-rise was a strange and friendly place, and that it was a fine thing on arriving there to find another rise to go over. It may very well be that she now needed someone to love, for loving is a most receiving thing, as anyone can attest who has been loved without returning it. It is the one who is loved who must give and give. And she found her love, not in her wandering, but at the market. The shape of her love, his colors and sounds, were so much with her that when she saw him first it was without surprise; and thereafter, for a very long while, it was quite enough that he lived. He gave to her by being alive, by setting the air athrum with his mighty voice, by his stride, which was, for a man afoot, the exact analog of what the horseman calls a "perfect seat."

After seeing him, of course, she received twice and twice again as much as ever before. A tree was straight and tall for the magnificent sake of being straight and tall, but wasn't straightness a part of him, and being tall? The oriole gave more now than song, and the hawk more than walking the wind, for had they not hearts like his, warm blood and his same striving to keep it so for tomorrow? And more and more, over-the-rise was the place for her, for only there could there be more and still more things like him.

But when she found the pure pool in the brackish Bogs, there was no more over-the-rise for her. It was a place without hardness or hate, where the aspens trembled only for wonder, and where all contentment was rewarded. Every single rabbit there was *the* champion nose-twinkler, and every waterbird could stand on one leg the longest, and proud of it. Shelf-fungi hung to the

125

willow-trunks, making that certain, single purple of which the sunset is incapable, and a tanager and a cardinal gravely granted one another his definition of "red."

Here Barbara brought a heart light with happiness, large with love, and set it down on the blue moss. And since the loving heart can receive more than anything else, so it is most needed, and Barbara took the best bird songs, and the richest colors, and the deepest peace, and all the other things which are most worth giving. The chipmunks brought her nuts when she was hungry and the prettiest stones when she was not. A green snake explained to her, in pantomime, how a river of jewels may flow uphill, and three mad otters described how a bundle of joy may slip and slide down and down and be all the more joyful for it. And there was the magic moment when a midge hovered, and then a honeybee, and then a bumblebee, and at last a hummingbird; and there they hung, playing a chord in A sharp minor.

Then one day the pool fell silent, and Barbara learned why the water was pure.

The aspens stopped trembling.

The rabbits all came out of the thicket and clustered on the bank, backs straight, ears up, and all their noses as still as coral.

The waterbirds stepped backwards, like courtiers, and stopped on the brink with their heads turned side-wise, one eye closed, the better to see with the other.

The chipmunks respectfully emptied their cheek pouches, scrubbed their paws together and tucked them out of sight; then stood still as tent pegs.

The pressure of growth around the pool ceased: the very grass waited.

The last sound of all to be heard—and by then it was

very quiet—was the soft *whick!* of an owl's eyelids as it awoke to watch.

He came like a cloud, the earth cupping itself to take each of his golden hooves. He stopped on the bank and lowered his head, and for a brief moment his eyes met Barbara's, and she looked into a second universe of wisdom and compassion. Then there was the arch of the magnificent neck, the blinding flash of his golden horn.

And he drank, and he was gone. Everyone knows the water is pure, where the unicorn drinks.

How long had he been there? How long gone? Did time wait too, like the grass?

"And couldn't he stay?" she wept. "Couldn't he stay?"

To have seen the unicorn is a sad thing; one might never see him more. But then—to have seen the unicorn!

She began to make a song.

It was late when Barbara came in from the Bogs, so late the moon was bleached with cold and fleeing to the horizon. She struck the highroad just below the Great House and turned to pass it and go out to her garden house.

Near the locked main gate an animal was barking. A sick animal, a big animal. . . .

Barbara could see in the dark better than most, and soon saw the creature clinging to the gate, climbing, uttering that coughing moan as it went. At the top it slipped, fell outward, dangled; then there was a ripping sound, and it fell heavily to the ground and lay still and quiet.

She ran to it, and it began to make the sound again. It was a man, and he was weeping.

It was her love, her love, who was tall and straight and so very alive—her love, battered and bleeding, puffy, broken, his clothes torn, crying.

Now of all times was the time for a lover to receive, to take from the loved one his pain, his trouble, his fear. "Oh, hush, hush," she whispered, her hands touching his bruised face like swift feathers. "It's all over now. It's all over."

She turned him over on his back and knelt to bring him up sitting. She lifted one of his thick arms around her shoulder. He was very heavy, but she was very strong. When he was upright, gasping weakly, she looked up and down the road in the waning moonlight. Nothing, no one. The Great House was dark. Across the road, though, was a meadow with high hedgerows which might break the wind a little.

"Come, my love, my dear love," she whispered. He trembled violently.

All but carrying him, she got him across the road, over the shallow ditch, and through a gap in the hedge. She almost fell with him there. She gritted her teeth and set him down gently. She let him lean against the hedge, and then ran and swept up great armfuls of sweet broom. She made a tight springy bundle of it and set it on the ground beside him, and put a corner of her cloak over it, and gently lowered his head until it was pillowed. She folded the rest of the cloak about him. He was very cold.

There was no water near, and she dared not leave him. With her kerchief she cleaned some of the blood from his face. He was still very cold. He said, "You devil. You rotten little devil."

"Shh." She crept in beside him and cradled his head. "You'll be warm in a minute."

"Stand still," he growled. "You keep running away."

"I won't run away," she whispered. "Oh, my darling, you've been hurt, so hurt. I won't leave you. I promise I won't leave you."

He lay very still. He made the growling sound again.

"I'll tell you a lovely thing," she said softly. "Listen to me, think about the lovely thing," she crooned.

"There's a place in the bog, a pool of pure water, where the trees live beautifully, willow and aspen and birch, where everything is peaceful, my darling, and the flowers grow without tearing their petals. The moss is blue and the water is like diamonds."

"You tell me stories in a thousand voices," he muttered.

"Shh. Listen, my darling. This isn't a story, it's a real place. Four miles north and a little west, and you can see the trees from the ridge with the two dwarf oaks. And I know why the water is pure!" she cried gladly. "I know why!"

He said nothing. He took a deep breath and it hurt him, for he shuddered painfully.

"The unicorn drinks there," she whispered. "I *saw* him!"

Still he said nothing. She said, "I made a song about it. Listen, this is the song I made:

And He—suddenly gleamed! My dazzled eyes,
Coming from outer sunshine to this green
And secret gloaming, met without surprise
The vision. Only after, when the sheen
And splendor of his going fled away,
I knew amazement, wonder and despair,
That he should come—and pass—and would not stay,
The Silken-swift—the gloriously Fair!
That he should come—and pass—and would not stay,
So that, forever after, I must go,
Take the long road that mounts against the day,
Travelling in the hope that I shall know

Again that lifted moment, high and sweet,
Somewhere—on purple moor or windy hill—
Remembering still his wild and delicate feet,
The magic and the dream—remembering still!

His breathing was more regular. She said, "I truly *saw* him!"

"I'm blind," he said. "Blind, I'm blind."

"Oh, my dear. . . ."

He fumbled for her hand, found it. For a long moment he held it. Then, slowly, he brought up his other hand and with them both he felt her hand, turned it about, squeezed it. Suddenly he grunted, half sitting. "You're here!"

"Of course, darling. Of course I'm here."

"Why?" he shouted. "Why? *Why?* Why all of this? Why blind me?" He sat up, mouthing, and put his great hand on her throat. "Why do all that if. . . ." The words ran together into an animal noise. Wine and witchery, anger and agony boiled in his veins.

Once she cried out.

Once she sobbed.

"Now," he said, "you'll catch no unicorns. Get away from me." He cuffed her.

"You're mad. You're sick," she cried.

"Get away," he said ominously.

Terrified, she rose. He took the cloak and hurled it after her. It almost toppled her as she ran away, crying silently.

After a long time, from behind the hedge, the sick, coughing sobs began again.

Three weeks later Rita was in the market when a hard hand took her upper arm and pressed her into the angle of a cottage wall. She did not start. She flashed her eyes upward and recognized him, and then said composedly, "Don't touch me."

"I need you to tell me something," he said. "And tell me you *will!*" His voice was as hard as his hand.

"I'll tell you anything you like," she said. "But don't touch me."

He hesitated, then released her. She turned to him casually. "What is it?" Her gaze darted across his face and its almost-healed scars. The small smile tugged at one corner of her mouth.

His eyes were slits. "I have to know this: why did you make up all that . . . prettiness, that food, that poison . . . just for me? You could have had me for less."

She smiled. "Just for you? It was your turn, that's all."

He was genuinely surprised. "It's happened before?"

She nodded. "Whenever it's the full of the moon—and the squire's away."

"You're lying!"

"You forget yourself!" she said sharply. Then, smiling, "It is the truth, though."

"I'd've heard talk—"

"Would you now? And tell me—how many of your friends know about your humiliating adventure?"

He hung his head.

She nodded. "You see? They go away until they're healed, and they come back and say nothing. And they always will."

"You're a devil . . . why do you do it? Why?"

"I told you," she said openly. "I'm a woman and I act like a woman in my own way. No man will ever touch me, though. I am virgin and shall remain so."

"You're *what?*" he roared.

She held up a restraining, ladylike glove. "Please," she said, pained.

"Listen," he said, quietly now, but with such intensity that for once she stepped back a pace. He closed his eyes, thinking hard. "You told me—the pool, the pool of the unicorn, and a song, wait. 'The Silken-swift, the gloriously Fair . . .' Remember? And then I—I saw to it that *you'd* never catch a unicorn!"

She shook her head, complete candor in her face. "I like that, 'the Silken-swift.' Pretty. But believe me—no! That isn't mine."

He put his face close to hers, and though it was barely a whisper, it came out like bullets. "Liar! Liar! I couldn't forget. I was sick, I was hurt, I was poisoned, but I know what I did!" He turned on his heel and strode away.

She put the thumb of her glove against her upper teeth for a second, then ran after him. "Del!"

He stopped but, rudely, would not turn. She rounded him, faced him. "I'll not have you believing that of me—it's the one thing I have left," she said tremulously.

He made no attempt to conceal his surprise. She controlled her expression with a visible effort, and said, "Please. Tell me a little more—just about the pool, the song, whatever it was."

"You don't remember?"

"I don't *know*!" she flashed. She was deeply agitated.

He said with mock patience, "You told me of a unicorn pool out on the Bogs. You said you had seen *him* drink there. You made a song about it. And then I—"

"Where? Where was this?"

"You forget so soon?"

"Where? Where did it happen?"

"In the meadow, across the road from your gate, where you followed me," he said. "Where my sight came back to me, when the sun came up."

She looked at him blankly, and slowly her face changed. First the imprisoned smile struggling to be

132

free, and then—she was herself again, and she laughed. She laughed a great ringing peal of the laughter that had plagued him so, and she did not stop until he put one hand behind his back, then the other, and she saw his shoulders swell with the effort to keep from striking her dead.

"You animal!" she said, goodhumoredly. "Do you know what you've done? Oh, you . . . you *animal!*" She glanced around to see that there were no ears to hear her. "I left you at the foot of the terrace steps," she told him. Her eyes sparkled. "Inside the gates, you understand? And you. . . ."

"Don't laugh," he said quietly.

She did not laugh. "That was someone else out there. Who, I can't imagine. But it wasn't I."

He paled. "You followed me out."

"On my soul I did not," she said soberly. Then she quelled another laugh.

"That can't be," he said. "I couldn't have. . . ."

"But you were blind, blind and crazy, Del-my-lover!"

"Squire's daughter, take care," he hissed. Then he pulled his big hand through his hair. "It can't be. It's three weeks; I'd have been accused. . . ."

"There are those who wouldn't," she smiled. "Or—perhaps she will, in time."

"There has never been a woman so foul," he said evenly, looking her straight in the eye. "You're lying—you know you're lying."

"What must I do to prove it—aside from that which I'll have no man do?"

His lip curled. "Catch the unicorn," he said.

"If I did, you'd believe I was virgin?"

"I must," he admitted. He turned away, then said, over his shoulder, "But—*you?*"

She watched him thoughtfully until he left the

marketplace. Her eyes sparkled; then she walked briskly to the goldsmith's, where she ordered a bridle of woven gold.

If the unicorn pool lay in the Bogs nearby, Rita reasoned, someone who was familiar with that brackish wasteland must know of it. And when she made a list in her mind of those few who travelled the Bogs, she knew whom to ask. With that, the other deduction came readily. Her laughter drew stares as she moved through the marketplace.

By the vegetable stall she stopped. The girl looked up patiently.

Rita stood swinging one expensive glove against the other wrist, half-smiling. "So you're the one." She studied the plain, inward-turning, peaceful face until Barbara had to turn her eyes away. Rita said, without further preamble, "I want you to show me the unicorn pool in two weeks."

Barbara looked up again, and now it was Rita who dropped her eyes. Rita said, "I can have someone else find it, of course. If you'd rather not." She spoke very clearly, and people turned to listen. They looked from Barbara to Rita and back again, and they waited.

"I don't mind," said Barbara faintly. As soon as Rita had left, smiling, she packed up her things and went silently back to her house.

The goldsmith, of course, made no secret of such an extraordinary commission; and that, plus the gossips who had overheard Rita talking to Barbara, made the expedition into a cavalcade. The whole village turned out to see; the boys kept firmly in check so that Rita might lead the way; the young bloods ranged behind her (some a little less carefree than they might be) and others snickering behind their hands. Behind them the girls, one or two a little pale, others eager as cats to see the squire's daughter fall, and perhaps even . . . but then, only she had the golden bridle.

She carried it casually, but casualness could not hide it, for it was not wrapped, and it swung and blazed in the sun. She wore a flowing white robe, trimmed a little short so that she might negotiate the rough bogland; she had on a golden girdle and little gold sandals, and a gold chain bound her head and hair like a coronet.

Barbara walked quietly a little behind Rita, closed in with her own thoughts. Not once did she look at Del, who strode somberly by himself.

Rita halted a moment and let Barbara catch up, then walked beside her. "Tell me," she said quietly, "why did you come? It needn't have been you."

"I'm his friend," Barbara said. She quickly touched the bridle with her finger. "The unicorn."

"Oh," said Rita. "The unicorn." She looked archly at the other girl. "You wouldn't betray all your friends, would you?"

Barbara looked at her thoughtfully, without anger. "If—when you catch the unicorn," she said carefully, "what will you do with him?"

"What an amazing question! I shall keep him, of course!"

"I thought I might persuade you to let him go."

Rita smiled, and hung the bridle on her other arm. "You could never do that."

"I know," said Barbara. "But I thought I might, so that's why I came." And before Rita could answer, she dropped behind again.

The last ridge, the one which overlooked the unicorn

pool, saw a series of gasps as the ranks of villagers topped it, one after the other, and saw what lay below; and it was indeed beautiful.

Surprisingly, it was Del who took it upon himself to call out, in his great voice, "Everyone wait here!" And everyone did; the top of the ridge filled slowly, from one side to the other, with craning, murmuring people. And then Del bounded after Rita and Barbara.

Barbara said, "I'll stop here."

"Wait," said Rita, imperiously. Of Del she demanded, "What are you coming for?"

"To see fair play," he growled. "The little I know of witchcraft makes me like none of it."

"Very well," she said calmly. Then she smiled her very own smile. "Since you insist, I'd rather enjoy Barbara's company too."

Barbara hesitated. "Come, he won't hurt you, girl," said Rita. "He doesn't know you exist."

"Oh," said Barbara, wonderingly.

Del said gruffly, "I do so. She has the vegetable stall."

Rita smiled at Barbara, the secrets bright in her eyes. Barbara said nothing, but came with them.

"You should go back, you know," Rita said silkily to Del, when she could. "Haven't you been humiliated enough yet?"

He did not answer.

She said, "Stubborn animal! Do you think I'd have come this far if I weren't sure?"

"Yes," said Del, "I think perhaps you would."

They reached the blue moss. Rita shuffled it about with her feet and then sank gracefully down to it. Barbara stood alone in the shadows of the willow grove. Del thumped gently at an aspen with his fist. Rita, smiling, arranged the bridle to cast, and laid it across her lap.

The rabbits stayed hid. There was an uneasiness

about the grove. Barbara sank to her knees, and put out her hand. A chipmunk ran to nestle in it.

This time there was a difference. This time it was not the slow silencing of living things that warned of his approach, but a sudden babble from the people on the ridge.

Rita gathered her legs under her like a sprinter, and held the bridle poised. Her eyes were round and bright, and the tip of her tongue showed between her white teeth. Barbara was a statue. Del put his back against his tree, and became as still as Barbara.

Then from the ridge came a single, simultaneous intake of breath, and silence. One knew without looking that some stared speechless, that some buried their faces or threw an arm over their eyes.

He came.

He came slowly this time, his golden hooves choosing his paces like so many embroidery needles. He held his splendid head high. He regarded the three on the bank gravely, and then turned to look at the ridge for a moment. At last he turned, and came round the pond by the willow grove. Just on the blue moss, he stopped to look down into the pond. It seemed that he drew one deep clear breath. He bent his head then, and drank, and lifted his head to shake away the shining drops.

He turned toward the three spellbound humans and looked at them each in turn. And it was not Rita he went to, at last, nor Barbara. He came to Del, and he drank of Del's eyes with his own just as he had partaken of the pool—deeply and at leisure. The beauty and wisdom were there, and the compassion, and what looked like a bright white point of anger. Del knew that the creature had read everything then, and that he knew all three of them in ways unknown to human beings.

There was a majestic sadness in the way he turned

then, and dropped his shining head, and stepped daintily to Rita. She sighed, and rose up a little, lifting the bridle. The unicorn lowered his horn to receive it—

—and tossed his head, tore the bridle out of her grasp, sent the golden thing high in the air. It turned there in the sun, and fell into the pond.

And the instant it touched the water, the pond was a bog and the birds rose mourning from the trees. The unicorn looked up at them, and shook himself. Then he trotted to Barbara and knelt, and put his smooth, stainless head in her lap.

Barbara's hands stayed on the ground by her sides. Her gaze roved over the warm white beauty, up to the tip of the golden horn and back.

The scream was frightening. Rita's hands were up like claws, and she had bitten her tongue; there was blood on her mouth. She screamed again. She threw herself off the now withered moss toward the unicorn and Barbara. "She can't be!" Rita shrieked. She collided with Del's broad right hand. "It's wrong, I tell you, she, you, I. . . ."

"I'm satisfied," said Del, low in his throat. "Keep away, squire's daughter."

She recoiled from him, made as if to try to circle him. He stepped forward. She ground her chin into one shoulder, then the other, in a gesture of sheer frustration, turned suddenly and ran toward the ridge. "It's mine, it's mine," she screamed. "I tell you it can't be hers, don't you understand? I never once, I never did, but she, but she—"

She slowed and stopped, then, and fell silent at the sound that rose from the ridge. It began like the first patter of rain on oak leaves, and it gathered voice until it was a rumble and then a roar. She stood looking up, her face working, the sound washing over her. She shrank from it.

It was laughter.

She turned once, a pleading just beginning to form on her face. Del regarded her stonily. She faced the ridge then, and squared her shoulders, and walked up the hill, to go into the laughter, to go through it, to have it follow her all the way home and all the days of her life.

Del turned to Barbara just as she bent over the beautiful head. She said, "Silken-swift . . . go free."

The unicorn raised its head and looked up at Del. Del's mouth opened. He took a clumsy step forward, stopped again. *"You!"*

Barbara's face was wet. "You weren't to know," she choked. "You weren't ever to know . . . I was so glad you were blind, because I thought you'd never know."

He fell on his knees beside her. And when he did, the unicorn touched her face with his satin nose, and all the girl's pent-up beauty flooded outward. The unicorn rose from his kneeling, and whickered softly. Del looked at her, and only the unicorn was more beautiful. He put out his hand to the shining neck, and for a moment felt the incredible silk of the mane flowing across his fingers. The unicorn reared then, and wheeled, and in a great leap was across the bog, and in two more was on the crest of the farther ridge. He paused there briefly, with the sun on him, and then was gone.

Barbara said, "For us, he lost his pool, his beautiful pool."

And Del said, "He will get another. He must." With difficulty he added, "He couldn't be . . . punished . . . for being so gloriously Fair."

V · THE ROC

The roc (or rukh) is a fabulous bird generally resembling an eagle, a bird so big and strong that it is capable of carrying an elephant off in its talons. And, as legend has it, the elephants the roc carried off served to feed its young. Modern research indicates that the legend of the roc is not a purely imaginary fable, but portrays an actual bird in exaggerated guise. Very large birds, now extinct, such as *Aepyornis maximus,* a giant relative of the ostrich, existed as recently as the seventeenth century on the island of Madagascar. *Aepyornis,* the largest bird that ever lived, reached a height of ten feet, and may well have been magnified in the telling by Marco Polo's informant.

Marco Polo refers to this giant bird as "the bird Gryphon," but he remarks that the island people call it the "Ruc" and makes it quite clear that it is not the griffin, which we have already met. Apparently Marco Polo never saw the roc himself, but only heard about it from informants who had visited Madagascar. However, its existence was generally accepted throughout the East.

Here, from *The Book of Marco Polo,* is a description of this legendary bird.

Marco Polo

THE ENORMOUS BIRD OF MADEIGASCAR

Madeigascar is an Island towards the south, about a thousand miles from Scotra. . . . And you must know that it is a most noble and beautiful Island, and one of the greatest in the world, for it is about four thousand miles in compass. The people live by trade and handicrafts. . . . You must know that this Island lies so far south that ships cannot go further south or visit other Islands in that direction, except this one, and that other of which we have to tell you, called Zanzibar. This is because the sea-current runs so strong towards the south that the ships which should attempt it never would get back again. . . .

'Tis said that in those other Islands to the south, which the ships are unable to visit because this strong current prevents their return, is found the bird *Gryphon,* which appears there at certain seasons. The description given of it is however entirely different from what our stories and pictures make it. For persons who had been there and had seen it told Messer Marco Polo that it was for all the world like an eagle, but one indeed of enormous size; so big in fact that its wings covered an extent of thirty paces, and its quills were twelve paces long, and thick in proportion. And it is so strong that it will seize an elephant in its talons and carry him high into the air, and drop him so that he is smashed to pieces; having so killed him the bird gryphon swoops down on him and eats him at leisure. The people of those isles call the bird *Ruc,* and it has no other name. So I wot not if this be the

142

real gryphon, or if there be another manner of bird as
great. But this I can tell you for certain, that they are not
half lion and half bird as our stories do relate; but enormous as they be they are fashioned just like an eagle. . . .

Another famous traveler who told of his encounters with the roc—and exciting encounters they
were—was Sindbad the Sailor. Here, from the *Arabian
Nights,* is an account of Sindbad's second voyage and
of his adventures with this giant bird, whose egg he
mistook for the dome of a mosque.

Alf Laylah wa Laylah

THE SECOND VOYAGE OF SINDBAD THE SEAMAN

I was living a most enjoyable life until one day my mind
became possessed with the thought of travelling about
the world of men and seeing their cities and islands; and
a longing seized me to traffic and to make money by trade.
Upon this resolve I took a great store of cash and, buying
goods and gear fit for travel, bound them up in bales.
Then I went down to the river-bank, where I found a
noble ship and brand-new about to sail, equipped with
sails of fine cloth and well manned and provided; so I
took passage in her, with a number of other merchants,
and after embarking our goods we weighed anchor the
same day. Right fair was our voyage and we sailed from
place to place and from isle to isle; and whenever we
anchored we met a crowd of merchants and notables and
customers, and we took to buying and selling and barter-
ing. At last Destiny brought us to an island, fair and
verdant, in trees abundant, with yellow-ripe fruits luxuri-

ant, and flowers fragrant and birds warbling soft descant;
and streams crystalline and radiant; but no sign of man
showed to the descrier, no, not a blower of the fire. The
captain made fast with us to this island, and the merchants
and sailors landed and walked about, enjoying the shade
of the trees and the song of the birds, that chanted the
praises of the One, the Victorious, and marvelling at the
works of the Omnipotent King. I landed with the rest;
and, sitting down by a spring of sweet water that welled
up among the trees, took out some vivers I had with me
and ate of that which Allah Almighty had allotted unto
me. And so sweet was the zephyr and so fragrant were the
flowers, that presently I waxed drowsy and, lying down
in that place, was soon drowned in sleep. When I awoke,
I found myself alone, for the ship had sailed and left me
behind, nor had one of the merchants or sailors bethought
himself of me. I searched the island right and left, but
found neither man nor Jinn, whereat I was beyond measure troubled and my gall was like to burst for stress of
chagrin and anguish and concern, because I was left quite
alone, without aught of worldly gear or meat or drink,
weary and heartbroken. So I gave myself up for lost and
said, "Not always doth the crock escape the shock. I was
saved the first time by finding one who brought me from
the desert island to an inhabited place, but now there is
no hope for me." Then I fell to weeping and wailing and
gave myself up to an access of rage, blaming myself for
having again ventured upon the perils and hardships of
voyage, whenas I was at my ease in mine own house in
mine own land, taking my pleasure with good meat and
good drink and good clothes and lacking nothing, neither
money nor goods. And I repented me of having left
Baghdad, and this the more after all the travails and
dangers I had undergone in my first voyage, wherein I
had so narrowly escaped destruction, and exclaimed

"Verily we are Allah's and unto Him we are returning!"
I was indeed even as one mad and Jinn-struck and presently I rose and walked about the island, right and left
and every whither, unable for trouble to sit or tarry in
any one place. Then I climbed a tall tree and looked in
all directions, but saw nothing save sky and sea and trees
and birds and isles and sands. However, after a while my
eager glances fell upon some great white thing, afar off in
the interior of the island; so I came down from the tree
and made for that which I had seen; and behold, it was
a huge white dome rising high in air and of vast compass.
I walked all around it, but found no door thereto, nor
could I muster strength or nimbleness by reason of its
exceeding smoothness and slipperiness. So I marked the
spot where I stood and went round about the dome to
measure its circumference, which I found fifty good paces.
And as I stood, casting about how to gain an entrance,
the day being near its fall and the sun being near the
horizon, behold, the sun was suddenly hidden from me
and the air became dull and dark. Methought a cloud
had come over the sun, but it was the season of summer;
so I marvelled at this and lifting my head looked steadfastly at the sky, when I saw that the cloud was none other
than an enormous bird, of gigantic girth and inordinately
wide of wing which, as it flew through the air, veiled the
sun and hid it from the island. At this sight my wonder
redoubled and I remembered a story I had heard aforetime of pilgrims and travellers, how in a certain island
dwelleth a huge bird, called the "Rukh," which feedeth
its young on elephants; and I was certified that the dome
which caught my sight was none other than a Rukh's egg.
As I looked and wondered at the marvellous works of
the Almighty, the bird alighted on the dome and brooded
over it with its wings covering it and its legs stretched
out behind it on the ground, and in this posture it fell

asleep, glory be to Him who sleepeth not! When I saw
this, I arose and, unwinding my turband from my head,
doubled it and twisted it into a rope, with which I girt
my middle and bound my waist fast to the legs of the
Rukh, saying to myself, "Peradventure, this bird may
carry me to a land of cities and inhabitants, and that will
be better than abiding in this desert island." I passed the
night watching and fearing to sleep, lest the bird should
fly away with me unawares; and, as soon as the dawn
broke and morn shone, the Rukh rose off its egg and,
spreading its wings with a great cry, flew up into the air,
dragging me with it; nor ceased it to soar and to tower
till I thought it had reached the limit of the firmament;
after which it descended, earthwards, little by little, till
it lighted on the top of a high hill. As soon as I found
myself on the hard ground, I made haste to unbind myself, quaking for fear of the bird, though it took no heed
of me nor even felt me; and, loosing my turband from its
feet, I made off with my best speed. Presently, I saw it
catch up in its huge claws something from the earth and
rise with it high in air, and observing it narrowly I saw
it to be a serpent big of bulk and gigantic of girth, wherewith it flew away clean out of sight. I marvelled at this
and faring forwards found myself on a peak overlooking
a valley, exceeding great and wide and deep, and bounded
by vast mountains that spired high in air: none could
descry their summits, for the excess of their height, nor
was any able to climb up thereto. When I saw this, I
blamed myself for that which I had done and said,
"Would Heaven I had tarried in the island! It was better
than this wild desert; for there I had at least fruits to eat
and water to drink, and here are neither trees nor fruits
nor streams. But there is no Majesty and there is no
Might save in Allah, the Glorious, the Great! Verily, as

often as I am quit of one peril, I fall into a worse danger and a more grievous." However, I took courage and walking along the Wady found that its soil was of diamond, the stone wherewith they pierce minerals and precious stones and porcelain and the onyx, for that it is a dense stone and a dure, whereon neither iron nor hardhead hath effect, neither can we cut off aught therefrom nor break it, save by means of leadstone. Moreover, the valley swarmed with snakes and vipers, each big as a palm tree, that would have made but one gulp of an elephant; and they came out by night, hiding during the day, lest the Rukhs and eagles pounce on them and tear them to pieces, as was their wont, why I wot not. And I repented of what I had done and said, "By Allah, I have made haste to bring destruction upon myself!" The day began to wane as I went along and I looked about for a place where I might pass the night, being in fear of the serpents; and I took no thought of meat and drink in my concern for my life. Presently, I caught sight of a cave nearhand, with a narrow doorway; so I entered and, seeing a great stone close to the mouth, I rolled it up and stopped the entrance, saying to myself, "I am safe here for the night; and as soon as it is day, I will go forth and see what destiny will do." Then I looked within the cave and saw at the upper end a great serpent brooding on her eggs, at which my flesh quaked and my hair stood on end; but I raised my eyes to Heaven and, committing my case to fate and lot, abode all that night without sleep till daybreak, when I rolled back the stone from the mouth of the cave and went forth, staggering like a drunken man and giddy with watching and fear and hunger. As in this sore case I walked along the valley, behold, there fell down before me a slaughtered beast; but I saw no one, whereat I marvelled with great marvel and presently

147

remembered a story I had heard aforetime of traders and pilgrims and travellers; how the mountains where are the diamonds are full of perils and terrors, nor can any fare through them; but the merchants who traffic in diamonds have a device by which they obtain them, that is to say, they take a sheep and slaughter and skin it and cut it in pieces and cast them down from the mountain-tops into the valley-sole, where the meat being fresh and sticky with blood, some of the gems cleave to it. There they leave it till midday, when the eagles and vultures swoop down upon it and carry it in their claws to the mountain-summits, whereupon the merchants come and shout at them and scare them away from the meat. Then they come and, taking the diamonds which they find sticking to it, go their ways with them and leave the meat to the birds and beasts; nor can any come at the diamonds but by this device. So, when I saw the slaughtered beast fall and bethought me of the story, I went up to it and filled my pockets and shawl-girdle and turband and the folds of my clothes with the choicest diamonds; and, as I was thus engaged, down fell before me another great piece of meat. Then with my unrolled turband and lying on my back, I set the bit on my breast so that I was hidden by the meat, which was thus raised above the ground. Hardly had I gripped it, when an eagle swooped down upon the flesh and, seizing it with his talons, flew up with it high in air and me clinging thereto, and ceased not its flight till it alighted on the head of one of the mountains where, dropping the carcass he fell to rending it; but, behold, there arose behind him a great noise of shouting and clattering of wood, whereat the bird took fright and flew away. Then I loosed off myself the meat, with clothes daubed with blood therefrom, and stood by its side; whereupon up came the merchant, who had cried out at the eagle, and seeing me standing there, bespoke me not, but was affrighted at me and shook with fear. However, he went up to the carcass and turning it over, found no diamonds sticking to it, whereat he gave a great cry and exclaimed, "Harrow, my disappointment! There is no Majesty and there is no Might save in Allah, with whom we seek refuge from Satan the stoned!" And he bemoaned himself and beat hand upon hand, saying, "Alas, the pity of it! How cometh this?" Then I went up to him and he said to me, "Who art thou and what causeth thee to come hither?" And I, "Fear not, I am a man and a good man and a merchant. My story is wondrous and my adventures marvellous and the manner of my coming hither is prodigious. So be of good cheer, thou shalt receive of me what shall rejoice thee, for I have with me great plenty of diamonds and I will give thee thereof what shall suffice thee; for each is better than aught thou couldst get otherwise. So fear nothing." The man rejoiced thereat and thanked and blessed me; then we talked together till the other merchants, hearing me in discourse with their fellow, came up and saluted me; for each of them had thrown down his piece of meat. And as I went off with them I told them my whole story, how I had suffered hardships at sea and the fashion of my reaching the valley. But I gave the owner of the meat a number of the stones I had by me, so they all wished me joy of my escape, saying, "By Allah a new life hath been decreed to thee, for none ever reached yonder valley and came off thence alive before thee; but praised be Allah for thy safety!" We passed the night together in a safe and pleasant place, beyond measure rejoiced at my deliverance from the Valley of Serpents and my arrival in an inhabited land; and on the morrow we set out and journeyed over the mighty range of mountains, seeing many serpents in the valley, till we came to a fair great island, wherein was a garden of huge camphor trees, under each of which an hundred men might take shelter. When the folk have a mind to get camphor, they bore into the upper part of the bole with a long iron; whereupon the liquid camphor, which is the sap of the tree, floweth out and they catch it in vessels, where it concreteth like gum; but, after this, the tree dieth and becometh firewood. Moreover, there is in this island a kind of wild beast, called "Rhinoceros," that pastureth as do steers and buffalos with us; but it is a huge brute, bigger of body than the camel and like it feedeth upon the leaves and twigs of trees. It is a remarkable animal with a great and thick horn, ten cubits long, amiddleward its head; wherein, when cleft in twain, is the likeness of a man. Voyagers and pilgrims and travellers declare that this beast, called "Karkadan," will carry off a great elephant on its horn and graze about the island and the seacoast therewith and take no heed of it, till the elephant dieth and its fat, melting in the sun, runneth down into the rhinoceros's eyes and blindeth him, so that he lieth down on the shore. Then comes the bird Rukh and carrieth off both the rhinoceros and that which is on its horn to feed its young withal. Moreover, I saw in this island many kinds of oxen and buffalos, whose like are not found in our country. Here I sold some of the diamonds which I had by me for gold dinars and silver dirhams and bartered others for the produce of the country; and, loading them upon beasts of burden, fared on with the merchants from valley to valley and town to town, buying and selling and viewing foreign countries and the works and creatures of Allah, till we came to Bassorah-city, where we abode a few days, after which I continued my journey to Baghdad.

Next comes a modern tale of the adventures of some skeptical scientists in quest of the roc. The story is "Bird in the Hand," by Californian science-fiction writer Larry Niven.

Larry Niven

BIRD IN THE HAND

"It's not a roc," said Ra Chen.

The bird looked stupidly back at them from behind a thick glass wall. Its wings were small and underdeveloped; its legs and feet were tremendous, ludicrous. It weighed three hundred pounds and stood nearly eight feet tall.

Other than that, it looked a lot like a baby chick.

"It kicked me," Svetz complained. A slender, small-boned man, he stood stiffly this day, with a slight list to port. "It kicked me in the side and broke four ribs. I barely made it back to the extension cage."

"It still isn't a roc. Sorry about that, Svetz. We did some research in the history section of the Beverly Hills Library while you were in the hospital. The roc was only a legend."

"But look at it!"

Svetz's beefy, red-faced boss nodded. "That's probably what started the legend. Early explorers in Australia saw these—*ostriches* wandering about. They said to themselves, 'If the chicks are this size, what are the adults like?' Then they went home and told stories about the adults."

"I got my ribs caved in for a flightless bird?"

"Cheer up, Svetz. It's not a total loss. The ostrich was extinct. It makes a fine addition to the Secretary-General's vivarium."

"But the Secretary-General wanted a roc. What are you going to tell him?"

Ra Chen scowled. "It's worse than that. Do you know what the Secretary-General wants now?"

People meeting Ra Chen for the first time thought he was constantly scowling, until they saw his *scowl*: Svetz had suspected Ra Chen was worried. Now he knew it.

The Secretary-General was everybody's problem. A recessive gene inherited from his powerful, inbred family had left him with the intelligence of a six-year-old child. Another kind of inheritance had made him overlord of the Earth and its colonies. His whim was law throughout the explored universe.

Whatever the Secretary-General wanted now, it was vital that he get it.

"Some idiot took him diving in Los Angeles," Ra Chen said. "Now he insists on seeing the city before it sank."

"That doesn't sound too bad."

"It wouldn't be, if it had stopped there. Some of his Circle of Advisors noticed his interest, and they got him historical tapes on Los Angeles. He loved it. He wants to join the first Watts Riot."

Svetz gulped. "That should raise some security problems."

"The Secretary-General is as close to being pure Caucasian as makes no difference."

The ostrich cocked its head to one side, studying them. It still looked like the tremendous chick of an even bigger bird. Svetz could imagine that it had just cracked its way out of an egg the size of a bungalow.

"I'm going to have a headache," he said. "Why do you tell me these things? You *know* I have no head for politics."

"Can you imagine what would happen if we caused the death of the Secretary-General? Already there are powerful factions that would like to see the Institute for Temporal Research disbanded. Space, for instance, they'd *love* to swallow us up."

"But what can we do? We can't turn down a direct request from the Secretary-General!"

"We can distract him."

They had lowered their voices to conspiratorial whispers. Now they turned away from the ostrich and strolled casually down the line of glass cages.

"How?"

"I don't know yet. If I could only get to his nurse," Ra Chen said between his teeth. "I've tried hard enough. Maybe ISR has bought her. Maybe she's loyal. She's been with him thirty-eight years.

"How do I know what would catch the attention of the Secretary-General? I've only met him four times on formal occasions. I do know his attention span is low. If we could distract him with a new toy, he'd forget about Los Angeles."

The cage they were passing was labeled:

ELEPHANT
Retrieved from the year 700 AnteAtomic,
approximately, from the region of India, Earth,

EXTINCT

The wrinkled grey beast watched them go by with sleepy indifference. He had not been captured by Svetz.

But Svetz had captured almost half of the animals here, including several whose tanks were half full of water. Svetz was afraid of animals. Especially big animals. Why did Ra Chen keep sending him after animals?

The thirty feet of lizard in the next cage definitely

recognized Svetz. It jetted orange-white flame at him and flapped its tiny bat-like wings in fury when the flame washed harmlessly across the glass. If it ever got out—

But that was why the cages were airtight. The animals of Earth's past must be protected from the air of Earth's present.

Svetz remembered the cobalt-blue sky of Earth's past and was reassured. Today's afternoon sky was brilliant turquoise at the zenith, shading through pastel green and yellow to rich yellow-brown near the horizon. Svetz saw it and was reassured. If the Chinese fire-breather ever got out, it would be too busy gasping for purer air to attack Svetz.

"What can we get him? I think he's tired of these animals. Svetz, what about a giraffe?"

"A what?"

"Or a dog, or a satyr . . . it's got to be unusual," Ra Chen muttered. "A teddy bear?"

Out of his fear of animals, Svetz ventured, "I wonder if you might not be on the wrong track, sir."

"Mph? Why?"

"The Secretary-General has enough animals to satisfy a thousand men. Worse than that, you're competing with Space when you bring back funny animals. They can do that too."

Ra Chen scratched behind his ear. "I never thought of that. You're right. But we've got to do *something*."

"There must be lots of things to do with a time machine."

They could have taken a displacement plate back to the Center. Ra Chen preferred to walk. It would give him a chance to think, he said.

Svetz walked with bowed head and blind eyes along-side his boss. Inspiration had come to him at similar times, when he needed it. But they had reached the red sandstone cube that was the Center, and the mental lightning had not struck.

A big hand closed on his upper arm. "Just a minute," Ra Chen said softly. "The Secretary-General's paying us a visit."

Svetz's heart lurched. "How do you know?"

Ra Chen pointed. "You should recognize that thing on the walkway. We brought it back last month from Los Angeles, June third, twenty-six PostAtomic, the day of the Great California Earthquake. It's an internal combustion automobile. It belongs to the Secretary-General."

"What'll we do?"

"Go in and show him around," Ra Chen said grimly. "Pray he doesn't insist on being taken back to Watts, August eleventh, twenty PostAtomic."

"Suppose he does?"

"I'll have to send him back. Oh, not with you, Svetz. With Zeera. She's black, and she speaks american. It might help."

"Not enough," said Svetz, but he was already calmer. Let Zeera take the risks.

They passed close by the Secretary-General's automobile. Svetz was intrigued by its odd, angular look, its complex control panels, the shiny chrome trim. Someone had removed the hood, so that the polished complexity of the motor was open to view.

"Wait," Svetz said suddenly. "Does he like it?"

"*Will* you come on?"

"Does the Secretary-General like his automobile?"

"Sure, Svetz. He loves it."

"Get him another car. California must have been full of automobiles on the day before the Great Quake."

Ra Chen stopped suddenly. "That could be it. It would hold him for a while, give us time. . . ."

"Time for what?"

Ra Chen didn't hear. "A racing car . . . ? No, he'd kill himself. The Circle of Advisors would want to install a robot chauffer-override. Maybe a dune buggy?"

"Why not ask him?"

"It's worth a try," said Ra Chen. They went up the steps.

In the Center there were three time machines, including the one with the big extension cage, plus a host of panels with flashing colored lights. The Secretary-General liked those. He smiled and chuckled as Ra Chen led him about. His guards hovered at his shoulders, their faces stiff, their fingernails clicking against their gun butts.

Ra Chen introduced Svetz as "my best agent." Svetz was so overwhelmed by the honor he could only stutter. But the Secretary-General didn't seem to notice.

Whether he had forgotten about seeing the Watts Riot was moot, but he did forget to ask on that occasion.

When Ra Chen asked about cars, the Secretary-General smiled all across his face and nodded vigorously. Faced by a vast array of choices, five or six decades with dozens of new models for every year, the Secretary-General put his finger in his mouth and considered well.

Then he made his choice.

" 'Why not ask him? Why not ask him?' " Ra Chen mimicked savagely. "Now we know. The first car! He wants the first car ever made!"

"I thought he'd ask for a *make* of car." Svetz rubbed his eyes hard. "How can we possibly find one car? A couple of decades to search through, and all of the North American and European continents!"

"It's not that bad. We'll use the books from the Beverly Hills Library. But it's bad enough, Svetz. . . ."

The raid on the Beverly Hills Library had been launched in full daylight, using the big extension cage and a dozen guards armed with stunners, on June third, twenty-six PostAtomic. Giant time machines, crazy men wearing flying belts—on any other day it would have made every newspaper and television program in the country. But June the third was a kind of Happy Hunting Ground for the Institute for Temporal Research.

No Californian would report the raid, except to other Californians. If the story did get out, it would be swamped by more important news. The series of quakes would begin at sunset . . . had begun at sunset. . . .

Svetz and Ra Chen and Zeera Southworth spent half the night going through the history section of the Beverly Hills Library. Ra Chen knew enough white american to recognize titles, but in the end Zeera had to do the reading.

Zeera Southworth was tall and slender and very dark, crowned with hair like a black powder explosion. Among men who worked at the Center she was reputed to be as frigid as the caves of Pluto. She was also the only one who could handle the unique horned horse Svetz had brought back from prehistoric Britain.

She sat gracefully cross-legged, reading pertinent sections aloud, while the others paced. They followed a twisting trail of references. . . .

By two in the morning they were damp and furious.

"Nobody invented the automobile!" Ra Chen exploded. "It just happened!"

"We certainly have a wide range of choices," Zeera agreed. "I take it we won't want any of the steam automobiles. That would eliminate Cugnot and Trevithick and the later British steam coaches."

"Thank Science for eliminating *something*."

Svetz said, "Our best bets seem to be Lenoir of France

and Marcus of Vienna. Except that Daimler and Benz have good claims, and Selden's patent held good for years—"

"Dammit, pick one!"

"Just a minute, sir." Zeera alone retained some semblance of calm. "This Ford might be the best we've got."

"Ford? Why? He invented nothing but a system of mass production."

Zeera held up the book. Svetz recognized it: a biography she had been reading earlier. "This book implies that Ford was responsible for everything, that he created the automobile industry single-handed."

"But we know that isn't true," Svetz protested.

Ra Chen made a pushing motion with one hand. "Let's not be hasty. We take Ford's car, and we produce that book to authenticate it. Who'll know the difference?"

"But if someone does the same research we just—oh. Sure. He'll get the same answers. No answers. Ford's just as good a choice as any."

"Better, if nobody looks further," Zeera said with satisfaction. "Too bad we can't take the Model T; it looks much more like an automobile. This thing he started with looks like a kiddy cart. It says he built it out of old pipes."

"Tough," said Ra Chen.

Late the next morning, Ra Chen delivered last minute instructions.

"You can't just take the car," he told Zeera. "If you're interrupted, come back without it."

"Yes, sir. It would be less crucial if we took our duplicate from a later time, from the Smithsonian Institute, for instance."

"The automobile has to be new. Be reasonable, Zeera!

We can't give the Secretary-General a second-hand automobile!"

"No, sir."

"We'll land you about three in the morning. Use infrared and pills to change your vision. Don't show any visible light. Artificial light would probably scare them silly."

"Right."

"Were you shown—"

"I know how to use the duplicator." Zeera sounded faintly supercilious, as always. "I also know that it reverses the image."

"Never mind that. Bring back the reversed duplicate, and we'll just reverse it again."

"Of course." She seemed chagrined that she had not seen that for herself. "What about dialect?"

"You speak black and white american, but it's for a later period. Don't use slang. Stick to black unless you want to impress someone white. Then speak white, but speak slowly and carefully and use simple words. They'll think you're from another country. I hope."

Zeera nodded crisply. She stooped and entered the extension cage, turned and pulled the duplicator after her. Its bulk was small, but it weighed a ton or so without the lift field generator to float it. One end glowed white with glow-paint.

They watched the extension cage blur and vanish. It was still attached to the rest of the time machine, but attached along a direction that did not transmit light.

"Now then!" Ra Chen rubbed his hands together. "I don't expect she'll have any trouble getting Henry Ford's flightless flight stick. Our trouble may come when the Secretary-General sees what he's got."

Svetz nodded, remembering the grey-and-flat pictures

in the history books. Ford's machine was ungainly, slip-shod, ugly and undependable. A few small surreptitious additions would make it dependable enough to suit the Secretary-General. *Nothing* would make it beautiful.

"We need another distraction," said Ra Chen. "We've only bought ourselves more time to get it."

Zeera's small time machine gave off a sound of ripping cloth, subdued, monotonous, reassuring. A dozen workmen were readying the big extension cage. Zeera would need it to transport the duplicate automobile.

"There's something I'd like to try," Svetz ventured.

"Concerning what?"

"The roc."

Ra Chen grinned. "The ostrich, you mean. Don't you ever give up? There wasn't any roc, Svetz."

Svetz looked stubborn. "Do you know anything about neoteny?"

"Never heard of it. Look, Svetz, we're going to be over budget because of the roc trip. Not your fault, of course, but another trip would cost us over a million commercials, and—"

"I don't need the time machine."

"Oh?"

"I would like the help of the Palace Veterinarian. Have you got enough pull for that?"

The Palace Veterinarian was a stocky, blocky, busty woman with muscular legs and a thrusting jaw. A floating platform packed with equipment followed her between the rows of cages.

"I know every one of these beasts," she told Svetz. "Once I even thought of giving them names. An animal ought to have a name."

"They've got names."

"That's what I decided. GILA MONSTER, ELEPHANT, OSTRICH," she read. "You give Gilgamesh a name so he won't get mixed up with Gilbert. But nobody would get HORSE mixed up with ELEPHANT. There's only one of each. It's sad."

"There are the clones."

"Do you know what we do with the clones? We let them grow to infancy, then freeze 'em. Only one at a time of each species is alive." She stopped before the cage marked OSTRICH. "Is this your prize? I've been meaning to come see him."

The bird shifted its feet in indecision; it cocked its head to consider the couple on the other side of the glass. It seemed surprised at Svetz's return.

"He looks just like a newly hatched chick," she said. "Except for the legs and feet, of course. They seem to have developed to support the extra mass."

Svetz was edgy with the need to be in two places at once. His own suggestion had sparked Zeera's project. He ought to be there. Yet—the ostrich had been his first failure.

He asked, "Does it look neotenous?"

"Neotenous? Obviously. Neoteny is a common method of evolution. We have neotenous traits ourselves, you know. Bare skin, where all the other primates are covered with hair. When our ancestors started chasing their meat across the plains, they needed a better cooling system than most primates need. So they kept one aspect of immaturity, the bare skin.

"The axolotl was a classic example of neoteny—"

"The what?"

"You know what a salamander was, don't you? It had gills and fins while immature. As an adult it grew lungs and shed the gills and lived on land. The axolotl was a viable offshoot that never lost the gills and fins. A gene shift. Typical of neoteny."

"I never heard of either, axolotls or salamanders."

"They've been extinct for a long time. They needed open streams and ponds to live."

Svetz nodded. Open water was deadly poison, anywhere on Earth.

"The problem is that we don't know when your bird lost its ability to fly. Some random neotenous development may have occurred far in the past, so that the bird's wings never developed. Then it may have evolved its present size to compensate."

"Oh. Then the ancestor—"

"May have been no bigger than a turkey. Shall we go in and look?"

The glass irised open to admit them. Svetz stepped into the cage, felt the tug of the pressure curtain flowing over and around him. The ostrich backed warily away.

The vet opened a pouch on her floating platform, withdrew a stunner, and used it. The ostrich squawked in outrage and collapsed. No muss, no fuss.

The vet strode toward her patient—and stopped suddenly in the middle of the cage. She sniffed, sniffed again in horror. "Have I lost my sense of smell?"

Svetz produced two items like cellophane bags, handed her one. "Put this on."

"Why?"

"You might suffocate if you don't." He donned the other himself, by pulling it over his head, then pressing the rim against the skin of his neck. It stuck. When he finished he had a hermetic seal.

"This air is deadly," he explained. "It's the air of the Earth's past, reconstituted. Think of it as coming from fifteen hundred years ago. There were so few men then that they might as well have never discovered fire, as far as the composition of the air was concerned. That's why

162

you don't smell anything but ostrich. Nothing's been burned yet."

"You don't need sulphur dioxide and carbon monoxide to keep you alive. You do need carbon dioxide. A certain concentration of carbon dioxide in your blood activates the breathing reflex."

She had finished donning her filter helmet. "I take it the concentration is too low in here."

"Right. You'd forget to breathe. You're used to air that's four percent carbon dioxide. In here it's barely a tenth of that.

"The bird can breathe this bland stuff. In fact, it'd die without it. What we've put into the air in the past fifteen hundred years, we've had fifteen hundred years to adapt to. The ostrich hasn't."

"I'll keep that in mind," she said shortly, so that Svetz wondered if he'd been lecturing someone who knew more than he did. She knelt beside the sleeping ostrich, and the platform floated lower for her convenience.

Svetz watched her as she ministered to the ostrich, taking tissue samples, testing blood pressure and heartbeat in reaction to small doses of hormones and drugs.

In a general way he knew what she was doing. There were techniques for reversing the most recent mutations in an animal's genetic make-up. One did not always get what one expected. Still—there was a *homo habilis* several cages down, who had been in the Circle of Advisors until he called the Secretary-General a tyrannical fugghead.

While she was identifying the neotenous developments, she would also be trying to guess what she would have when they were eliminated. Then there were matters of metabolism. If Svetz was right, the bird's mass would increase rapidly. It must be fed intravenously, and even more rapidly.

In general—but the details of what she was doing were mysterious and dull.

Svetz found himself studying her filter helmet. Full inflation had rendered it almost invisible. A golden rim of it showed by diffraction against the yellow-brown sky.

Did Space really want to take over the Institute for Temporal Research? Then that golden halo was support for their claim. It was a semipermeable membrane. It would selectively pass gases in both directions in such a way as to make an almost breathable atmosphere breathable.

It had been taken unchanged from a Space warehouse.

Other ITR equipment had come from the space industries. Flight sticks. Anesthetic needle guns. The low mass antigravity unit in the new extension cage.

But their basic argument was more subtle.

Once the ocean teemed with life, Svetz thought. *Now the continental shelf is as dead as the Moon: nothing but bubble cities. Once this whole continent was all forest and living desert and fresh water. We cut down the trees and shot the animals and poisoned the rivers and irrigated the deserts so that even the desert life had died, and now there's nothing left but the food yeast and us.*

We've forgotten so much about the past that we can't separate legend from fact. We've wiped out most of the forms of life on Earth in the last fifteen hundred years, and changed the composition of the air to the extent that we'd be afraid to change it back.

I fear the unknown beasts of the past. I cannot breathe the air. I cannot recognize the edible plants. I would not kill animals for food. I don't know which would kill me.

The Earth's past is as foreign to me as another planet.

The Palace Veterinarian was busy hooking the ostrich intravenously to tubing of several colors.

Svetz's pocket phone rang.

For a wild moment Svetz considered not answering. But good manners won out, and Svetz opened the phone.

"There's trouble," said Ra Chen's image. "Zeera's cage is on its way back. She must have pulled the go-home lever right after she called for the big extension cage."

"She left before the big cage could get there?"

"Yah," said Ra Chen. "Whatever happened must have happened fast. If she called for the big cage, then she had the automobile. A moment later she aborted the mission. Svetz, I'm worried."

"I'd hate to leave now, sir." Svetz turned to look at the ostrich. In that moment all of the bird's feathers fell out, leaving it plump and naked.

That decided him. "I can't leave now, sir. We'll have a full-grown roc in a few minutes."

"What? *Good!* But how?"

"The ostrich was a neotenous offshoot of the roc. We've produced a throwback."

"Good! Stick with it, Svetz. We'll handle it here." Ra Chen switched off.

The Palace Veterinarian said, "You shouldn't make promises you can't keep."

Svetz's heart leapt. "Trouble?"

"No. It's going beautifully so far."

"All the feathers fell out. Is that good?"

"Don't worry about it. See for yourself: already there's a coat of down. Your ostrich is reverting to chickhood," she said cheerfully. "Its ancestor's chickhood. If the ancestor really was no bigger than a turkey before it lost the ability to fly, it'll be even smaller as a chick."

"What'll happen then?"

"It'll drown in its own fat."

"We should have taken a clone."

"Too late. Look at it now, look at the legs. They aren't nearly as overdeveloped."

The bird was a big ball of pale yellow down. Its frame had shrunk, but its legs had shrunk much more. Standing, it would have been no more than four feet tall. The extra mass had turned to fat, so that the ostrich was nearly spherical; it bulged like a poolside toy, lying on its inflated side in a pool of feathers.

"Now it *really* looks like a chick," said Svetz.

"It does, Svetz. In fact, it is. That was a *big* chick. The adult is going to be tremendous." The Palace Veterinarian jumped to her feet. "Svetz, we've got to hurry. Is there a basic yeast source in this cage?"

"Sure. Why?"

"He'll starve at the rate he's growing, unless . . . just show me, Svetz."

The animals of the Zoo ate yeast, like everyone else, but with special additives for each animal. A brain tap could induce the animal to imagine it was eating whatever it was used to eating when the time probe had picked it up.

Svetz showed her the yeast tap. She hooked the pipeline to one of the machines on her floating platform; she made adaptions, added another machine. . . .

The bird grew visibly. Its fat layer shrank, deflated. Its legs and wings stretched outward. The beak began to take a distinctive hooked form, sharp and wicked looking.

Svetz began to feel panic. Beneath its downy feathers the bird was little more than taut skin stretched over long bones.

The yeast was now feeding directly into two tanks on the floating platform, and from there into the colored tubes. Somehow the Palace Veterinarian was converting the yeast directly into sugar-plasma.

"It's working now," she said. "I wasn't sure it would. He'll be all right now, if the growth cycle slows down in time." She smiled up at him. "You were right all along. The ostrich was a neotenous roc."

At that moment the light changed.

Svetz wasn't sure what had disturbed him. But he looked up—and the sky was baby blue from the horizon to the zenith.

"What is it?" The woman beside him was bemused rather than frightened. "I never saw a color like that in my life!"

"I have."

"What is it?"

"Don't worry about it. But keep your filter helmet on, especially if you have to leave the cage. Can you remember that?"

"Of course." Her eyes narrowed. "You know something about this, Svetz. It's something to do with time, isn't it?"

"I think so." Svetz used the key beam then, to avoid further questions from her. The glass peeled back to let him out.

He turned for a last look through the glass.

The Palace Veterinarian looked frightened. She must have guessed too much for her own comfort. But she turned away to care for her patient.

The ostrich lay on its side, its eyes open now. It was tremendous, and still scrawny despite the volume of the intravenous feed. Its feathers were changing color. The bird would be black and green.

It was half as big as the elephant next door . . .

whose air of grey wisdom was giving way to uneasiness as he watched.

It looked nothing like an ostrich.

The sky was baby blue, the blue of the deep past, crossed with fluffy clouds of clean and shining white. Blue from the horizon to the zenith, without a trace of the additives that ought to be there.

Unconscious men and women lay everywhere. Svetz dared not stop to help. What he had to do was more important.

He slowed to a walk as he neared the Center. There was pain like a knife blade inserted between his partly healed ribs.

ITR crewmen had fallen in the walkway around the Center, presumably after staggering outside. And there was the Secretary-General's automobile sitting quietly in front. Behind it, flat on his back, was Ra Chen.

What did he think he was doing there?

Svetz heard the purr of the motor as he approached. So that was it. Ra Chen must have hoped that the exhaust would revive him. Damn clever; and it should have worked. Why hadn't it?

Svetz looked into the polished metal guts of the motor as he passed. The motor had changed . . . somehow. What ran it now? Steam? Electricity? A flywheel? In any event, the exhaust pipe Ra Chen had been searching for was no longer there.

Ra Chen was alive, his pulse rapid and frantic. But he wasn't breathing. Or . . . yes, he was. He was breathing perhaps twice a minute as carbon dioxide built up enough to activate the reflex.

Svetz went on into the Center.

More than a dozen men and women had collapsed across lighted control panels. Three more figures sprawled in an aisle. The Secretary-General lay in angular disorder, smiling foolishly up at the ceiling. His guards wore troubled sleeping expressions and held drawn guns.

The small extension cage had not returned.

Svetz looked into the empty gap in the time machine, and felt terror. What could he accomplish without Zeera to tell him what had gone wrong?

From 50 AnteAtomic to the present was a thirty-minute trip. Ra Chen's call to the Zoo must have come less than thirty minutes ago. Weird, how an emergency could telescope time.

Unless that was a side effect of the paradox. Unless the paradox had chopped away Zeera's extension cage and left her stranded in the past, or cast off into an alternate world line, or. . . .

There had never been a temporal paradox.

Math was no help. The mathematics of time travel was riddled with singularities.

Last year somebody had tried to do a topological analysis of the path of an extension cage. He had proved not only that time travel was impossible, but that you couldn't travel faster than light either. Ra Chen had leaked the news to Space on the off chance that their hyperdrive ships would stop working.

What to do? Start putting filter helmets on everyone? Great, but the helmets weren't kept at the Center; he'd have to go across town. Did he dare leave the Center?

Svetz forced himself to sit down.

Minutes later, he snapped alert at the *pop* of displaced air. The small extension cage had returned. Zeera was crawling out of the circular doorway.

"Get back in there," Svetz ordered. "Quick!"

"I don't take orders from you, Svetz." She brushed past him and looked about her. "The automobile's gone.

Where's Ra Chen?" Zeera's face was blank with shock and exhaustion. Her voice was a monotone, ragged at the edges.

Svetz took her arm. "Zeera, we've—"

She jerked away. "We've got to *do* something. The automobile's gone. Didn't you hear me?"

"Did you hear *me*? Get back in the extension cage!"

"But we've got to decide what to *do*. Why can't I smell anything?" She sniffed at air that was scentless, empty, dead. She looked about herself in bewilderment, realizing for the first time just how strange everything was.

Then the eyes rolled up in her head, and Svetz stepped forward to catch her.

He studied her sleeping face across the diameter of the extension cage. It was very different from her waking face. Softer, more vulnerable. And prettier. Zeera had quite a pretty face.

"You should relax more often," he said.

His ribs throbbed where the ostrich had kicked him. The pain seemed to beat like a heart.

Zeera opened her eyes. She asked, "Why are we in here?"

"The extension cage has its own air system," said Svetz. "You can't breathe the outside air."

"Why not?"

"You tell me."

Her eyes went wide. "The automobile! It's gone!"

"Why?"

"I don't know, Svetz. I *swear* I did everything right. But when I turned on the duplicator the automobile disappeared!"

"That . . . doesn't sound at all good." Svetz strove to keep his voice level. "What did you—"

"I did it just the way they taught me! I hooked the glow-painted end to the frame, set the dials for an estimated mass plus a margin of error, read the dials off—"

"You must have hooked up the wrong end somehow. Wait a minute. Were you using the infrared flash?"

"Of course. It was dead of night."

"And you'd taken the pills so you'd be able to see infrared."

"Do you always think that slowly, Svetz?" Then her eyes changed, and Svetz knew she'd seen it. "I was seeing infrared. Of course. I hooked up the hot end."

"The duplicator end. Sure. That would duplicate empty space where there was an automobile. You'd get emptiness at both ends."

Zeera relaxed against the curved side of the extension cage, with her arms hooked under her knees. Presently she said, "Henry Ford sold that automobile for two hundred dollars, according to the book. Later he had trouble getting financed. Could the money have been crucial?"

"It must have been. How much is two hundred dollars?"

"Then someone else used mass production to make automobiles. And he must have liked steam or electricity."

"Steam, I'd guess. Steam came first."

"Tell me this, Svetz. If the air changed, why didn't we change with it? We evolved to be able to breathe air with a certain percentage of carbon monoxide and sulphur dioxide and nitrous and nitric oxides and so forth. Shouldn't the evolution have been canceled too? For that matter, who do we remember?"

"There's a lot we don't know about time travel. How do you expect logic to hold when paradoxes hold too?"

"Does that mean you don't know?"

171

"Yes."

"I'm not nagging, Svetz. I don't know either."

More silence.

"It's clear enough," Zeera said presently. "I'll have to go back and warn myself to get the duplicator on straight."

"That won't work. It didn't work. If you'd gotten the ends of the duplicator straight, we wouldn't be *in* this mess. Therefore you didn't."

She looked irritated. "Too logical. Well, what then?"

"Maybe we can go *around* you." Svetz hesitated, then plunged in. "Try this. Send me back to an hour before the earlier Zeera arrives. The automobile won't have disappeared yet. I'll duplicate it, duplicate the duplicate, take the reversed duplicate and the original automobile past you in the big extension cage. That lets you destroy the duplicate. I reappear after you're gone, leave the original automobile, and come back here with the reversed duplicate. How's that?"

"It sounded great. Would you mind going through it again?"

"Let's see. I go back to—"

She was laughing at him. "Never mind. But it has to be me, Svetz. You couldn't find your way. You couldn't ask directions or read the street signs. You'll have to stay here and man the machinery."

Reluctantly Svetz agreed.

They were leaving the extension cage when there came a scream like the end of the world.

Momentarily they froze. Then Svetz ran around the swelling flank of the cage. Zeera followed, wearing the filter helmet she had worn during her attempt to duplicate Ford's automobile.

172

One wall of the Center was glass. It framed a crest of hill across from the palace and a double row of cages that made up the Zoo. One of the cages was breaking apart as they watched, smashing itself to pieces like—

—Like an egg hatching. And like a chick emerging, the roc stood up in the ruin of its cage.

The scream came again.

"What is it?" Zeera whispered.

"It was an ostrich. I'd hate to give it a name now."

The bird seemed to move in slow motion. There was so much of it! Green and black, beautiful and evil, big as eternity, and a crest of golden feathers had sprouted on its forehead. Its hooked beak descended toward a cage.

That cage ripped like paper.

Zeera was shaking his arm. "Come on! If it came from the Zoo, we don't need to worry about it. It'll suffocate when we get the car back where it belongs."

"Oh. Right," said Svetz. They went to work moving the big extension cage a few hours further back in time.

When Svetz looked again, the bird was just taking to the air. Its wings flapped like sails, and their black shadows swept like cloud shadows over the houses. As the roc rose fully into view, Svetz saw that something writhed and struggled in its tremendous talons.

Svetz recognized it . . . and realized just how big the roc really was.

"It's got ELEPHANT," he said. An inexplicable sorrow gripped his heart; inexplicable, for Svetz hated animals.

"What? Come *on*, Svetz!"

"Um? Oh, yes." He helped Zeera into the small extension cage and sent it on its way.

Despite its sleeping crew, the machinery of the Center seemed to be working perfectly. If anything got off, Svetz would have six men's work to do. Therefore he prowled

173

among the control boards, alert for any discrepancy, making minor adjustments. . . . And occasionally he looked out the picture window.

The roc reached a tremendous height. Any ordinary bird would have been invisible long since. But the roc was all too visible, hovering in the blue sky while it killed and ate ELEPHANT.

Time passed.

Twenty minutes for Zeera to get back.

More time to make two duplicates of the automobile. Load them into the big extension cage. Then to signal Svetz—

The signal came. She had the cars; she wanted to be moved forward. Svetz played it safe and moved her forward six hours almost to dawn. She might be caught by an early riser, but at least Ford would have his automobile.

The roc had finished its bloody meal. ELEPHANT was gone, bones and all. And—Svetz watched until he was sure—the bird was dropping, riding down the sky on outstretched wings.

Svetz watched it grow bigger, and bigger yet, until it seemed to enfold the universe. It settled over the Center like a tornado cloud, in darkness and wind. Like twin tornado funnels, two sets of curved talons touched down in the walkway.

The bird bent low. An inhuman face looked in at Svetz through the picture window. It nearly filled the window.

It knows me, Svetz thought. Even a bird's brain must be intelligent in a head that size.

The vast head rose ponderously out of sight above the roof.

I had the ostrich. I should have been satisfied, thought

Svetz. *A coin in the hand is worth two in the street.* The ancient proverb could as easily be applied to birds.

The roof exploded downward around a tremendous hooked beak. Particles of concrete spattered against walls and floor. A yellow eye rolled and found Svetz, but the beak couldn't reach him. Not through *that* hole.

The head withdrew through the roof.

Three red lights. Svetz leapt for the board and began twisting dials. He made two lights turn green, then the third. It had not occurred to him to run. The bird would find him wherever he hid.

There! Zeera had pulled the go-home lever. From here it was all automatic.

Crash!

Svetz was backed up against the big time machine, pinned by a yellow eye as big as himself. Half the roof was gone, but still the bird's beak couldn't reach him. But a great talon came seeking him through the shattered glass.

The light changed.

Svetz sagged. Behind the green and black feathers he could see that the sky had turned pale yellow-green, marked with yellow-brown streamers of cloud.

The bird sniffed incredulously. It didn't have to be told twice. Its head rose through the ceiling; it stepped back from the Center for clearance; its great wings came down like thunderclouds.

Svetz stepped out to watch it rise.

He had to hug an ornamental pillar. The wind of its wings was a hurricane. The bird looked down once, and recognized him, and looked away.

It was still well in view, rising and circling, when Zeera stepped out to join him. Presently Ra Chen was there to follow their eyes. Then half the Center mainte-

nance team was gaping upward in awe and astonishment
. . . while the bird dwindled to a black shadow. Black
against pale green, climbing, climbing.

One sniff had been enough. The bird's brain was as
enormously proportioned as the rest of it. It had started
climbing immediately, without waiting to snatch up its
dessert.

Climbing, climbing toward the edge of space. Reaching for clean air.

The Secretary-General stood beside Svetz, smiling in
wonder, chuckling happily as he gazed upward.

Was the roc still climbing? No, the black shadow was
growing larger, sliding down the sky. And the slow
motion of the wings had stopped.

How was a roc to know that there was no clean air
anywhere?

VI · THE BASILISK

The basilisk, sometimes called the cockatrice, was one of the most widely feared monsters of the Middle Ages. It was quite small, as monsters go, but merely to cast eyes upon it meant certain death—the victim had no time even to give warning to his friends nearby. Even to hear it hiss was fatal. How we come to know what the basilisk looked like, if everyone who saw it expired on the spot, is a question that was never asked during its reign as the King of Serpents. The Greek and Roman writers who described it were respected authorities, and their opinions were accepted without doubt.

The basilisk has a strange life history, as do several of the mythical monsters. It was hatched by a serpent (some say a toad) from the egg laid by a nine-year-old cock (we must also not question how a male bird came to lay an egg). It had the head and winged body of the cock, and the tail of the serpent; it was said to be less than two-feet long, but was absolute monarch of the smaller reptiles, other snakes fleeing at the hiss of its approach.

Here is how Edward Topsell, the famous seventeenth-century naturalist, described the origin of the basilisk in his *History of Four-Footed Beasts.*

Edward Topsell

THE ORIGIN OF THE BASILISK

There is some question amongst Writers, about the generation of this Serpent: for some, (and those very many and learned) affirme him to be brought forth of a Cockes egge. For they say that when a Cocke groweth old, he layeth a certaine egge without any shell, instead whereof it is covered with a very thicke skinne, which is able to withstand the greatest force of an easie blow or fall. They say, moreover, that this Egge is layd onely in the Summer time, about the beginning of the Dogge-dayes, being not so long as a Hens Egge, but round and orbicular: Sometimes of a Foxie, sometimes of a yellowish muddy colour, which Egge is generated of the putrified seed of the Cocke, and afterward sat upon by a Snake or a Toad, bringeth forth the Cockatrice, being halfe a foot in length, the hinder part like a Snake, the former part like a Cocke, because of a treble combe on his forehead.

But the vulgar opinion of Europe is, that the Egge is nourished by a Toad, and not by a Snake; howbeit, in better experience it is found that the Cocke doth sit on that egge himselfe. . . .

Since the sight of a basilisk was deadly to all living creatures (the weasel seems to have been the only exception), a view of its own reflection in a mirror was equally deadly to the basilisk itself. This means of disposing of basilisks is credited, rightly or wrongly, to Aristotle. In almost all of the myths about this creature, a mirror or highly polished shield is the standard weapon of the basilisk hunt, with many a hunter losing his life because he forgot to keep his eyes closed when approaching the basilisk for the kill.

The legend of "The Vienna Basilisk," which follows, illustrates the excitement that develops when a basilisk comes to town.

Anonymous

THE VIENNA BASILISK

There was excitement outside Number 7 Schönlatern-gassc: a frenzied crowd of people, shouting, pointing, shoving, turning to one another to ask questions. The year was 1202; the place was the city of Vienna; the house was that of the master baker, Martin Garhibl. That morning the narrow street where Garhibl lived was full of townsfolk. They glared in fury at Garhibl's house and shook their fists at it; and in the front window the baker himself could be seen, glaring back at them just as angrily.

"The Lord should punish him!" someone cried.

"Bind him! Chain him! Send him to prison!" yelled another.

"It should have been Garhibl who saw the basilisk! He deserves it!"

At any moment the surging crowd might turn into a mob bent on riot. A dozen men pressed up close against the door of Number 7; there was talk of breaking it down and dragging Garhibl out. Suddenly a band of armed men pushed fiercely into the crowd: the city guards of Vienna, coming to restore order.

"Make way for the Master of Justice!" the guards

cried. "Make way for the law! Make way for Herr Jakob von der Hülben!"

The townspeople moved back as the guards, wielding pikestaffs and ungentle elbows, swiftly opened a path through the throng. Riding solemnly in their wake came Herr Jakob von der Hülben. The Master of Justice of Vienna was a dignified and impressive figure, wearing his high authority with much the same ease and assurance as he wore his costly robes of office. As he appeared, a few of the onlookers began to cry out, denouncing Garhibl and demanding that the baker be arrested and tried at once; but the Master of Justice withered them into silence with a cold, stern glance.

"Let Master Garhibl be brought forth," the Master of Justice commanded.

Two of the guards rapped on the baker's door. After a moment it opened, and Garhibl emerged. His face was reddened with rage and his eyes gleamed brightly; but the moment he saw Justice von der Hülben he gasped, covered his mouth, bowed his head in awe and fear.

It did not greatly surprise the Master of Justice that Garhibl should be in some sort of trouble. The baker was one of Vienna's least popular citizens—not that he sold stale bread, or gave false weight, but he was an arrogant, high-handed man, who gave himself airs and strode about the city as though he were a nobleman, and not merely a shopkeeper.

Coldly Justice von der Hülben said, "I pray you tell me, Master Garhibl, why all this uproar on your doorstep? And I caution you, it will be better for you if you remain close to the truth."

"I did nothing, Your Honor!" Garhibl cried, sputtering. "This riot is none of my doing! It was the basilisk—the basilisk in my well. But why blame me for the basilisk, I ask you?"

"Because you swore," a man nearby called out. "You caused the basilisk to appear!"

"Silence!" snapped the Master of Justice. "One voice at a time. Proceed, Master Garhibl."

Slowly, stumbling over his words, pausing more than once to exchange angry insults with members of the crowd, Garhibl told the story. It was all on account of the troubles he had with helpers and apprentices, he explained. They were forever leaving him after just a few weeks. The reason, said Garhibl, is that today's young people are flighty and undisciplined and lazy, more interested in their pleasures than in the rewards of hard work. (No, cried someone in the crowd. No one wants to work long for Master Garhibl because of his impossible temper and his immense greed!) At any rate, Garhibl went on, the only reliable apprentice he had had in quite awhile was a young man named Hans. But it seemed Hans stayed at his tasks not out of a fondness for work but rather out of love for the baker's beautiful golden-haired daughter, Apollonia. Garhibl knew nothing about this, of course— until the moment when Hans finally grew so bold as to ask for his daughter's hand in marriage.

Garhibl burst into a terrible rage and chased the apprentice through his house, shouting and gesticulating. How dare a mere apprentice, Garhibl demanded, hope to wed a girl of Apollonia's station and prospects in life? What impudence! What audacity! He pursued Hans to the front door, bellowing and cursing at every stride. As the terrified apprentice opened the door to flee, the sound of a crowing cock could be heard, for it was early in the morning when this encounter took place. "Go!" Garhibl roared. "And when that cock lays an egg—not before—you may return and ask again for Apollonia!"

All this took place some months ago. This very morning, Garhibl went on, his maidservant went to the well as usual at the time of cockcrow to fetch fresh water. As she lowered the bucket, the girl noticed a ghastly smell coming from below; and, peering over the edge of the well, she saw something glittering brightly in the depths. What had taken up residence in Master Garhibl's well? The girl told the tale to the baker, who sent his new apprentice down into the well to investigate. The boy climbed down the rope, gagging as he went, for the reek was indeed a fearsome one. Suddenly he gave a terrible cry; and Garhibl, rushing to look, saw the apprentice slumped, unconscious, against the rope. Hastily he hoisted the boy out of the well. In the fresh air the apprentice revived, but sat trembling for many minutes before he could describe what had frightened him so badly. There was a monster at the bottom of the well, he said, not great in size, but frightful in appearance: something like a serpent, but also somewhat like a rooster. Its eyes were as red and as fierce as fire, and on its head it wore a golden crown.

"A basilisk!" someone shouted. "Garhibl uttered a curse—and the cock's egg hatched into a basilisk!"

The Master of Justice nodded. Yes, surely it seemed that Garhibl, in his intemperate rage, had conjured a basilisk into being. Well, dealing with Garhibl was no great problem; he could be fined for his rashness, and the crowd would scatter. But how to deal with a basilisk? Who would rid Vienna of so deadly and sinister a creature? Already Justice von der Hülben could see the men of the city guard turning sideways and trying to look inconspicuous, as if fearing that they would be assigned the task of coping with the monster in Master Garhibl's well.

"Let a man of learning be brought," the Master of Justice ordered.

The city guards searched through Vienna and found

the city's wisest scholar, a man whose learning extended into every branch of knowledge. The scholar heard the story and said unhesitatingly, "Yes, yes, certainly, this is a basilisk. Aristotle speaks of him as the king of snakes— you know that *basileus* is the Greek word for king—and tells us to beware. Let the basilisk but breathe on a man, and that man will die. Nor can any weapon harm a basilisk."

"How, then, can we free our city from this monster?" the Master of Justice asked. "Is there no way?"

"Only one," the scholar replied. "You must know that the appearance of the basilisk is so horrifying that nothing can stand to behold it—not even the basilisk itself. Let it but see its own hideous form in a mirror, and it will die of fright!"

"A mirror," said the Master of Justice. "Let a mirror be fetched at once!"

"Of course," the scholar continued, "he who bears the mirror into the well runs a grave risk. If he fails to move swiftly and with vigor, he will fall victim to the basilisk's venom before the monster has seen itself in the mirror."

Justice von der Hülben, frowning, glanced about him. "Who will bear the mirror?" he asked, not really expecting anyone to answer and not at all certain what his next step would be. To his surprise there came a reply from the back of the crowd:

"I will bear the mirror!"

All heads turned. A young man with long yellow hair had spoken; and now he was coming forward, pale and tense but with a look of determination on his handsome face.

"Who is he?" people whispered. And others answered: "He is Hans, who was apprenticed to the baker!"

Hans it was. He stood before the Master of Justice,

who asked him again if he would carry the mirror into the well; and a second time Hans declared that he would.

"Take the mirror, then, Hans," said Herr von der Hülben. He glanced in Garhibl's direction and added, "If you destroy the basilisk, Apollonia is yours!"

Long afterward, when Vienna had been delivered from the dread basilisk and the wedding of Hans and Apollonia had been celebrated, an inscription was carved on a slab of stone that was mounted on the front of the house at Number 7 Schönlaterngasse. This is what it said:

ANNO DOMINI MCCII

Kaiser Friedrich II was elected. During his reign a basilisk sprung from a cock. It was like the effigy shown above and the well in which it was found was filled with soil, no doubt because many people died from the venom of the monster.

Renovated in 1677 by the landlord
Hanns Spannring, bookseller

The house where Master Garhibl lived was torn down long ago, and the inscription put up by Master Spannring the bookseller has likewise vanished. But the legend of the Basilisk of Vienna is still remembered in Austria.

VII · THE PHOENIX

Finally we come to the strangest and most wonderful of all mythical creatures—the phoenix. It is a magnificent bird, larger than an eagle, with a golden head, scarlet body, purple tail, and iridescent wings made up of feathers of many colors.

Legend tells us that there is never more than one phoenix at any time, and each time it dies, it is reborn from its own ashes. The phoenix is a long-lived bird—some say it lives five hundred years, some say a thousand, some say even more—and when the time comes for it to die, it flies home to Arabia. There the phoenix builds a nest in the top of the highest palm tree, loading it with aromatic spices like cinnamon and myrrh. At dawn it sings a sweet and haunting song to the sun, and as the sun pauses to listen, its first rays set fire to the nest. From the ashes of this fragrant fire the next phoenix, young and strong, rises to start the cycle anew.

This fantastic legend is at least as old as the mythology of ancient Egypt. The earliest known written reference to the phoenix appears in a fragmentary work of Hesiod, a Greek poet who lived about 800 B.C. The first detailed telling of the legend is found in the book of Herodotus, the great Greek historian of the fifth century B.C., who claims to have learned the tale from the priests of the sacred Egyptian city of Heliopolis (City of the Sun). Here is Herodotus' account.

Herodotus

THE SACRED BIRD OF HELIOPOLIS

They have also a sacred bird called the phoenix, which I myself have never seen, except in pictures. Indeed, it is a great rarity, even in Egypt, only coming there (according to the accounts of the people of Heliopolis) once in five hundred years, when the old phoenix dies. Its size and appearance, if it is like the pictures, are as follows: The plumage is partly red, partly golden, while the general make and size are almost exactly that of the eagle. They tell a story of what this bird does, which does not seem to me to be credible: that he comes all the way from Arabia, and brings the parent bird, all plastered over with myrrh, to the temple of the sun, and there buries the body. In order to bring him, they say, he first forms a ball of myrrh as big as he finds that he can carry; then he hollows out the ball, and puts his parent inside, after which he covers over the opening with fresh myrrh, and the ball is then of exactly the same weight as at first; so he brings it to Egypt, plastered over as I have said, and deposits it in the temple of the sun. Such is the story they tell of the doings of this bird.

E. Nesbit, a popular writer of children's stories of the early twentieth century, is famous for her tales of mythical monsters, particularly the dragon and the phoenix. Here, from her book *The Phoenix and the Carpet,* is the story of some children who play with fire and have the phoenix myth come to life before their very eyes.

E. Nesbit

THE EGG

It began with the day when it was almost the Fifth of November, and a doubt arose in some breast—Robert's, I fancy—as to the quality of the fireworks laid in for the Guy Fawkes celebration.

"They were jolly cheap," said whoever it was, and I think it was Robert, "and suppose they didn't go off on the night? Those Prosser kids would have something to snigger about then."

"The ones *I* got are all right," Jane said; "I know they are, because the man at the shop said they were worth thribble the money—"

"I'm sure thribble isn't grammar," Anthea said.

"Of course it isn't," said Cyril; "one word can't be grammar all by itself, so you needn't be so jolly clever."

Anthea was rummaging in the corner-drawers of her mind for a very disagreeable answer, when she remembered what a wet day it was, and how the boys had been disappointed of that ride to London and back on the top of the tram, which their mother had promised them as a reward for not having once forgotten, for six whole days, to wipe their boots on the mat when they came home from school.

So Anthea only said, "Don't be so jolly clever yourself, Squirrel. And the fireworks look all right, and you'll have the eightpence that your tram fares didn't cost today, to buy something more with. You ought to get a perfectly lovely Catharine wheel for eightpence."

"I daresay," said Cyril, coldly; "but it's not *your* eightpence anyhow—"

"But look here," said Robert, "really now, about the fireworks. We don't want to be disgraced before those kids next door. They think because they wear red plush on Sundays no one else is any good."

"I wouldn't wear plush if it was ever so—unless it was black to be beheaded in, if I was Mary Queen of Scots," said Anthea, with scorn.

Robert stuck steadily to his point. One great point about Robert is the steadiness with which he can stick.

"I think we ought to test them," he said.

"You young duffer," said Cyril, "fireworks are like postage stamps. You can only use them once."

"What do you suppose it means by 'Carter's tested seeds' in the advertisement?"

There was a blank silence. Then Cyril touched his forehead with his finger and shook his head.

"A little wrong here," he said. "I was always afraid of that with poor Robert. All that cleverness, you know, and being top in algebra so often—it's bound to tell—"

"Dry up," said Robert, fiercely. "Don't you see? You can't *test* seeds if you do them *all*. You just take a few here and there, and if those grow you can feel pretty sure the others will be—what do you call it?—Father told me— 'up to sample.' Don't you think we ought to sample the fireworks? Just shut our eyes and each draw one out, and then try them."

"But it's raining cats and dogs," said Jane.

"And Queen Anne is dead," rejoined Robert. No one was in a very good temper. "We needn't go out to do them; we can just move back the table, and let them off on the old tea-tray we play toboggans with. I don't know what *you* think, but *I* think it's time we did something, and that would be really useful; because then we shouldn't just *hope* the fireworks would make those Prossers sit up—we should *know*."

"It *would* be something to do," Cyril owned with languid approval.

So the table was moved back. And then the hole in the carpet, that had been near the window till the carpet was turned round, showed most awfully. But Anthea stole out on tip-toe, and got the tray when cook wasn't looking, and brought it in and put it over the hole.

Then all the fireworks were put on the table, and each of the four children shut its eyes very tight and put out its hand and grasped something. Robert took a cracker, Cyril and Anthea had Roman candles; but Jane's fat paw closed on the gem of the whole collection, the Jack-in-the-box that had cost two shillings, and one at least of the party—I will not say which, because it was sorry afterwards—declared that Jane had done it on purpose. Nobody was pleased. For the worst of it was that these four children, with a very proper dislike of anything even faintly bordering on the sneakish, had a law, unalterable as those of the Medes and Persians, that one had to stand by the results of a toss-up, or a drawing of lots, or any other appeal to chance, however much one might happen to dislike the way things were turning out.

"I didn't mean to," said Jane, near tears. "I don't care, I'll draw another—"

"You know jolly well you can't," said Cyril, bitterly. "It's settled. It's Medium and Persian. You've done it, and you'll have to stand by it—and us too, worse luck. Never mind. *You'*ll have your pocket-money before the Fifth. Anyway, we'll have the Jack-in-the-box *last,* and get the most out of it we can."

So the cracker and the Roman candles were lighted,

and they were all that could be expected for the money; but when it came to the Jack-in-the-box it simply sat in the tray and laughed at them, as Cyril said. They tried to light it with paper and they tried to light it with matches; they tried to light it with Vesuvian fusees from the pocket of father's second-best overcoat that was hanging in the hall. And then Anthea slipped away to the cupboard under the stairs where the brooms and dustpans were kept, and the rosiny fire-lighters that smell so nice and like the woods where pine trees grow, and the old newspapers, and the bees-wax and turpentine, and the horrid stiff dark rags that are used for cleaning brass and furniture, and the paraffin for the lamps. She came back with a little pot that had once cost sevenpence-halfpenny when it was full of red-currant jelly; but the jelly had been all eaten long ago, and now Anthea had filled the jar with paraffin. She came in, and she threw the paraffin over the tray just at the moment when Cyril was trying with the twenty-third match to light the Jack-in-the-box. The Jack-in-the-box did not catch fire any more than usual, but the paraffin acted quite differently, and in an instant a hot flash of flame leapt up and burnt off Cyril's eyelashes, and scorched the faces of all four before they could spring back. They backed, in four instantaneous bounds, as far as they could, which was to the wall, and the pillar of fire reached from floor to ceiling.

"My hat," said Cyril, with emotion, "you've done it this time, Anthea."

The flame was spreading out under the ceiling like the rose of fire in Mr. Rider Haggard's exciting story about Allan Quatermain. Robert and Cyril saw that no time was to be lost. They turned up the edges of the carpet, and kicked them over the tray. This cut off the column of fire, and it disappeared and there was nothing left but smoke and a dreadful smell of lamps that have been turned too low. All hands now rushed to the rescue, and the paraffin fire was only a bundle of trampled carpet, when suddenly a sharp crack beneath their feet made the amateur firemen start back. Another crack—the carpet moved as if it had had a cat wrapped in it; the Jack-in-the-box had at last allowed itself to be lighted, and it was going off with desperate violence inside the carpet.

Robert, with the air of one doing the only possible thing, rushed to the window and opened it. Anthea screamed, Jane burst into tears, and Cyril turned the table wrong way up on top of the carpet heap. But the firework went on, banging and bursting and spluttering even underneath the table.

Next moment mother rushed in, attracted by the howls of Anthea, and in a few moments the firework desisted and there was a dead silence, and the children stood looking at each other's black faces, and, out of the corners of their eyes, at mother's white one.

The fact that the nursery carpet was ruined occasioned but little surprise, nor was any one really astonished that bed should prove the immediate end of the adventure. It has been said that all roads lead to Rome; this may be true, but at any rate, in early youth I am quite sure that many roads lead to *bed*, and stop there—or *you* do.

The rest of the fireworks were confiscated, and mother was not pleased when father let them off himself in the back garden, though he said, "Well, how else can you get rid of them, my dear?"

You see, father had forgotten that the children were in disgrace, and that their bedroom windows looked out on to the back garden. So that they all saw the fireworks most beautifully, and admired the skill with which father handled them.

Next day all was forgotten and forgiven; only the

nursery had to be deeply cleaned (like spring-cleaning),
and the ceiling had to be whitewashed.

And mother went out; and just at tea-time next day
a man came with a rolled-up carpet, and father paid
him, and mother said—

"If the carpet isn't in good condition, you know, I
shall expect you to change it." And the man replied—

"There ain't a thread gone in it nowhere, mum. It's
a bargain, if ever there was one, and I'm more'n 'arf sorry
I let it go at the price; but we can't resist the lydies, can
we, sir?" and he winked at father and went away.

Then the carpet was put down in the nursery, and
sure enough there wasn't a hole in it anywhere.

As the last fold was unrolled something hard and
loud-sounding bumped out of it and trundled along the
nursery floor. All the children scrambled for it, and
Cyril got it. He took it to the gas. It was shaped like an
egg, very yellow and shiny, half-transparent, and it had
an odd sort of light in it that changed as you held it in
different ways. It was as though it was an egg with a yolk
of pale fire that just showed through the stone.

"I *may* keep it, mayn't I, mother?" Cyril asked. And
of course mother said no; they must take it back to the
man who had brought the carpet, because she had only
paid for a carpet, and not for a stone egg with a fiery
yolk to it.

So she told them where the shop was, and it was in
the Kentish Town Road, not far from the hotel that is
called the Bull and Gate. It was a poky little shop, and
the man was arranging furniture outside on the pavement
very cunningly, so that the more broken parts should
show as little as possible. And directly he saw the children
he knew them again, and he began at once, without
giving them a chance to speak.

"No you don't," he cried loudly; "I ain't a-goin' to

take back no carpets, so don't you make no bloomin'
errer. A bargain's a bargain, and the carpet's puffik
throughout."

"We don't want you to take it back," said Cyril; "but
we found something in it."

"It must have got into it up at your place, then," said
the man, with indignant promptness, "for there ain't
nothing in nothing as I sell. It's all as clean as a whistle."

"I never said it wasn't *clean*," said Cyril, "but—"

"Oh, if it's *moths*," said the man, "that's easy cured
with borax. But I expect it was only an odd one. I tell
you the carpet's good through and through. It hadn't got
no moths when it left my 'ands—not so much as an hegg."

"But that's just it," interrupted Jane; "there *was* so
much as an egg."

The man made a sort of rush at the children and
stamped his foot.

"Clear out, I say!" he shouted, "or I'll call for the
police. A nice thing for customers to 'ear you a-coming
'ere a-charging me with finding things in goods what I
sells. 'Ere, be off, afore I sends you off with a flea in your
ears. Hi! constable—"

The children fled, and they think, and their father
thinks, that they couldn't have done anything else.
Mother has her own opinion. But father said they might
keep the egg.

"The man certainly didn't know the egg was there
when he brought the carpet," said he, "any more than
your mother did, and we've as much right to it as he had."

So the egg was put on the mantelpiece, where it quite
brightened up the dingy nursery. The nursery was dingy,
because it was a basement room, and its windows looked
out on a stone area with a rockery made of clinkers facing
the windows. Nothing grew in the rockery except London
pride and snails.

The room had been described in the house agent's list as a "convenient breakfast-room in basement," and in the daytime it was rather dark. This did not matter so much in the evenings when the gas was alight, but then it was in the evening that the blackbeetles got so sociable, and used to come out of the low cupboards on each side of the fireplace where their homes were, and try to make friends with the children. At least, I suppose that was what they wanted, but the children never would.

On the Fifth of November father and mother went to the theatre, and the children were not happy, because the Prossers next door had lots of fireworks and they had none.

They were not even allowed to have a bonfire in the garden.

"No more playing with fire, thank you," was father's answer, when they asked him.

When the baby had been put to bed the children sat sadly round the fire in the nursery.

"I'm beastly bored," said Robert.

"Let's talk about the Psammead," said Anthea, who generally tried to give the conversation a cheerful turn.

"What's the good of *talking*?" said Cyril. "What I want is for something to happen. It's awfully stuffy for a chap not to be allowed out in the evenings. There's simply nothing to do when you've got through your homers."

Jane finished the last of her home-lessons and shut the book with a bang.

"We've got the pleasure of memory," said she. "Just think of last holidays."

Last holidays, indeed, offered something to think of —for they had been spent in the country at a white house between a sand-pit and a gravel-pit, and things had happened. The children had found a Psammead, or sand-fairy, and it had let them have anything they wished for —just exactly anything, with no bother about its not being really for their good, or anything like that. And if you want to know what kind of things they wished for, and how their wishes turned out you can read it all in a book called *Five Children and It* (*It* was the Psammead). If you've not read it, perhaps I ought to tell you that the fifth child was the baby brother, who was called the Lamb, because the first thing he ever said was "Baa!" and that the other children were not particularly hand-some, nor were they extra clever, nor extraordinarily good. But they were not bad sorts on the whole; in fact, they were rather like you.

"I don't want to think about the pleasures of mem-ory," said Cyril; "I want some more things to happen."

"We're very much luckier than any one else, as it is," said Jane. "Why, no one else ever found a Psammead. We ought to be grateful."

"Why shouldn't we *go on* being, though?" Cyril asked—"lucky, I mean; not grateful. Why's it all got to stop?"

"Perhaps something will happen," said Anthea, com-fortably. "Do you know, sometimes I think we are the sort of people that things *do* happen to."

"It's like that in history," said Jane: "some kings are full of interesting things, and others—nothing ever hap-pens to them, except their being born and crowned and buried, and sometimes not that."

"I think Panther's right," said Cyril: "I think we are the sort of people things do happen to. I have a sort of feeling things would happen right enough if we could only give them a shove. It just wants something to start it. That's all."

"I wish they taught magic at school," Jane sighed. "I believe if we could do a little magic it might make something happen."

"I wonder how you begin?" Robert looked round the room, but he got no ideas from the faded green curtains, or the drab Venetian blinds, or the worn brown oil-cloth on the floor. Even the new carpet suggested nothing, though its pattern was a very wonderful one, and always seemed as though it were just going to make you think of something.

"I could begin right enough," said Anthea; "I've read lots about it. But I believe it's wrong in the Bible."

"It's only wrong in the Bible because people wanted to hurt other people. I don't see how things can be wrong unless they hurt somebody, and we don't want to hurt anybody; and what's more, we jolly well couldn't if we tried. Let's get the *Ingoldsby Legends*. There's a thing about Abracadabra there," said Cyril, yawning. "We may as well play at magic. Let's be Knights Templars. They were awfully gone on magic. They used to work spells or something with a goat and a goose. Father says so."

"Well, that's all right," said Robert, unkindly; "you can play the goat right enough, and Jane knows how to be a goose."

"I'll get *Ingoldsby*," said Anthea, hastily. "You turn up the hearthrug."

So they traced strange figures on the linoleum, where the hearthrug had kept it clean. They traced them with chalk that Robert had nicked from the top of the mathematical master's desk at school. You know, of course, that it is stealing to take a new stick of chalk, but it is not wrong to take a broken piece, so long as you only take one. (I do not know the reason of this rule, nor who made it.) And they chanted all the gloomiest songs they could think of. And, of course, nothing happened. So then Anthea said, "I'm sure a magic fire ought to be made of sweet-smelling wood, and have magic gums and essences and things in it."

"I don't know any sweet-smelling wood, except cedar," said Robert; "but I've got some ends of cedar-wood lead pencil."

So they burned the ends of lead pencil. And still nothing happened.

"Let's burn some of the eucalyptus oil we have for our colds," said Anthea.

And they did. It certainly smelt very strong. And they burned lumps of camphor out of the big chest. It was very bright, and made a horrid black smoke, which looked very magical. But still nothing happened. Then they got some clean tea-cloths from the dresser drawer in the kitchen, and waved them over the magic chalk-tracings, and sang "The Hymn of the Moravian Nuns at Bethlehem," which is very impressive. And still nothing happened. So they waved more and more wildly, and Robert's tea-cloth caught the golden egg and whisked it off the mantelpiece, and it fell into the fender and rolled under the grate.

"Oh, crikey!" said more than one voice.

And every one instantly fell down flat on its front to look under the grate, and there lay the egg, glowing in a nest of hot ashes.

"It's not smashed, anyhow," said Robert, and he put his hand under the grate and picked up the egg. But the egg was much hotter than any one would have believed it could possibly get in such a short time, and Robert had to drop it with a cry of "Bother!" It fell on the top bar of the grate, and bounced right into the glowing red-hot heart of the fire.

"The tongs!" cried Anthea. But, alas, no one could

remember where they were. Every one had forgotten that the tongs had last been used to fish up the doll's teapot from the bottom of the water-butt, where the Lamb had dropped it. So the nursery tongs were resting between the water-butt and the dustbin, and cook refused to lend the kitchen ones.

"Never mind," said Robert, "we'll get it out with the poker and the shovel."

"Oh, stop," cried Anthea. "Look at it! Look! look! look! look! I do believe something *is* going to happen!"

For the egg was now red-hot, and inside it something was moving. Next moment there was a soft cracking sound; the egg burst in two, and out of it came a flame-colored bird. It rested a moment among the flames, and as it rested there the four children could see it growing bigger and bigger under their eyes.

Every mouth was agape, every eye a-goggle.

The bird rose in its nest of fire, stretched its wings, and flew out into the room. It flew round and round, and round again, and where it passed the air was warm. Then it perched on the fender. The children looked at each other. Then Cyril put out a hand towards the bird. It put its head on one side and looked up at him, as you may have seen a parrot do when it is just going to speak, so that the children were hardly astonished at all when it said, "Be careful; I am not nearly cool yet."

They were not astonished, but they were very, very much interested.

They looked at the bird, and it was certainly worth looking at. Its feathers were like gold. It was about as large as a bantam, only its beak was not at all bantam-shaped. "I believe I know what it it," said Robert. "I've seen a picture—"

He hurried away. A hasty dash and scramble among

the papers on father's study table yielded, as the sum-books say, "the desired result." But when he came back into the room holding out a paper, and crying, "I say, look here," the others all said "Hush!" and he hushed obediently and instantly, for the bird was speaking.

"Which of you," it was saying, "put the egg into the fire?"

"He did," said three voices, and three fingers pointed at Robert.

The bird bowed; at least it was more like that than anything else. "I am your grateful debtor," it said with a high-bred air.

The children were all choking with wonder and curiosity—all except Robert. He held the paper in his hand, and he *knew*. He said so. He said—

"*I* know who you are."

And he opened and displayed a printed paper, at the head of which was a little picture of a bird sitting in a nest of flames.

"You are the Phoenix," said Robert; and the bird was quite pleased.

"My fame has lived then for two thousand years," it said. "Allow me to look at my portrait."

It looked at the page which Robert, kneeling down, spread out in the fender, and said—

"It's not a flattering likeness. . . . And what are these characters?" it asked, pointing to the printed part.

"Oh, that's all dullish; it's not much about *you*, you know," said Cyril, with unconscious politeness; "but you're in lots of books—"

"With portraits?" asked the Phoenix.

"Well, no," said Cyril; "in fact, I don't think I ever saw any portrait of you but that one, but I can read you something about yourself, if you like."

The Phoenix nodded, and Cyril went off and fetched Volume X of the old *Encyclopedia,* and on page 246 he found the following:

"Phoenix—in ornithology, a fabulous bird of antiquity."

"Antiquity is quite correct," said the Phoenix, "but fabulous—well, do I look it?"

Every one shook its head. Cyril went on—

"The ancients speak of this bird as single, or the only one of its kind."

"That's right enough," said the Phoenix.

"They describe it as about the size of an eagle."

"Eagles are of different sizes," said the Phoenix; "it's not at all a good description."

All the children were kneeling on the hearthrug, to be as near the Phoenix as possible.

"You'll boil your brains," it said. "Look out, I'm nearly cool now"; and with a whirr of golden wings it fluttered from the fender to the table. It was so nearly cool that there was only a very faint smell of burning when it had settled itself on the table-cloth.

"It's only a very little scorched," said the Phoenix, apologetically; "it will come out in the wash. Please go on reading."

The children gathered round the table.

"The size of an eagle," Cyril went on, "its head finely crested with a beautiful plumage, its neck covered with feathers of a gold color, and the rest of its body purple; only the tail white, and the eyes sparkling like stars. They say that it lives about five hundred years in the wilderness, and when advanced in age it builds itself a pile of sweet wood and aromatic gums, fires it with the wafting of its wings, and thus burns itself; and that from its ashes arises a worm, which in time grows up to be a Phoenix. Hence the Phoenicians gave—"

"Never mind what they gave," said the Phoenix, ruffling its golden feathers. "They never gave much, anyway; they always were people who gave nothing for nothing. That book ought to be destroyed. It's most inaccurate. The rest of my body was *never* purple, and as for my tail—well, I simply ask you, *is* it white?"

It turned round and gravely presented its golden tail to the children.

"No, it's not," said everybody.

"No, and it never was," said the Phoenix. "And that about the worm is just a vulgar insult. The Phoenix has an egg, like all respectable birds. It makes a pile—that part's all right—and it lays its egg, and it burns itself; and it goes to sleep and wakes up in its egg, and comes out and goes on living again, and so on for ever and ever. I can't tell you how weary I got of it—such a restless existence; no repose."

"But how did your egg get *here?*" asked Anthea.

"Ah, that's my life-secret," said the Phoenix. "I couldn't tell it to any one who wasn't really sympathetic. I've always been a misunderstood bird. You can tell that by what they say about the worm. I might tell *you,*" it went on, looking at Robert with eyes that were indeed starry. "*You* put me on the fire—"

Robert looked uncomfortable.

"The rest of us made the fire of sweet-scented woods and gums, though," said Cyril.

"And— and it was an accident my putting you on the fire," said Robert, telling the truth with some difficulty, for he did not know how the Phoenix might take it. It took it in the most unexpected manner.

"Your candid avowal," it said, "removes my last scruple. I will tell you my story."

"And you won't vanish, or anything sudden, will you?" asked Anthea, anxiously.

"Why?" it asked, puffing out the golden feathers, "do you wish me to stay here?"

"Oh *yes*," said every one, with unmistakable sincerity.

"Why?" asked the Phoenix again, looking modestly at the table-cloth.

"Because," said every one at once, and then stopped short; only Jane added after a pause, "you are the most beautiful person we've ever seen."

"You are a sensible child," said the Phoenix, "and I will *not* vanish or anything sudden. And I will tell you my tale. I had resided, as your book says, for many thousand years in the wilderness, which is a large, quiet place with very little really good society, and I was becoming weary of the monotony of my existence. But I acquired the habit of laying my egg and burning myself every five hundred years—and you know how difficult it is to break yourself of a habit."

"Yes," said Cyril; "Jane used to bite her nails."

"But I broke myself of it," urged Jane, rather hurt, "you know I did."

"Not till they put bitter aloes on them," said Cyril.

"I doubt," said the bird, gravely, "whether even bitter aloes (the aloe, by the way, has a bad habit of its own, which it might well cure before seeking to cure others; I allude to its indolent practice of flowering but once a century), I doubt whether even bitter aloes could have cured *me*. But I *was* cured. I awoke one morning from a feverish dream—it was getting near the time for me to lay that tiresome fire and lay that tedious egg upon it— and I saw two people, a man and a woman. They were sitting on a carpet—and when I accosted them civilly they narrated to me their life-story, which, as you have not yet heard it, I will now proceed to relate. They were a prince and princess, and the story of their parents was one which I am sure you will like to hear. In early youth the mother of the princess happened to hear the story of a certain enchanter, and in that story I am sure you will be interested. The enchanter—"

"Oh, please don't," said Anthea. "I can't understand all these beginnings of stories, and you seem to be getting deeper and deeper in them every minute. Do tell us your *own* story. That's what we really want to hear."

"Well," said the Phoenix, seeming on the whole rather flattered, "to cut about seventy long stories short (though *I* had to listen to them all—but to be sure in the wilderness there is plenty of time), this prince and princess were so fond of each other that they did not want any one else, and the enchanter—don't be alarmed, I won't go into his history—had given them a magic carpet (you've heard of a magic carpet?), and they had just sat on it and told it to take them right away from every one—and it had brought them to the wilderness. And as they meant to stay there they had no further use for the carpet, so they gave it to me. That was indeed the chance of a lifetime!"

"I don't see what you wanted with a carpet," said Jane, "when you've got those lovely wings."

"They *are* nice wings, aren't they?" said the Phoenix, simpering and spreading them out. "Well, I got the prince to lay out the carpet, and I laid my egg on it; then I said to the carpet, 'Now, my excellent carpet, prove your worth. Take that egg somewhere where it can't be hatched for two thousand years, and where, when that time's up, some one will light a fire of sweet wood and aromatic gums, and put the egg in to hatch'; and you see it's all come out exactly as I said. The words were no sooner out of my beak than egg and carpet disappeared. The royal lovers assisted to arrange my pile, and soothed my last moments. I burnt myself up and knew no more till I awoke on yonder altar."

It pointed its claw at the grate.

"But the carpet," said Robert, "the magic carpet that takes you anywhere you wish. What became of that?"

"Oh, *that?*" said the Phoenix, carelessly—"I should say that that is the carpet. I remember the pattern perfectly."

It pointed as it spoke to the floor, where lay the carpet which mother had bought in the Kentish Town Road for twenty-two shillings and ninepence.

At that instant father's latch-key was heard in the door.

"*Oh,*" whispered Cyril, "now we shall catch it for not being in bed!"

"Wish yourself there," said the Phoenix, in a hurried whisper, "and then wish the carpet back in its place."

No sooner said than done. It made one a little giddy, certainly, and a little breathless; but when things seemed right way up again, there the children were, in bed, and the lights were out.

They heard the soft voice of the Phoenix through the darkness.

"I shall sleep on the cornice above your curtains," it said. "Please don't mention me to your kinsfolk."

"Not much good," said Robert, "they'd never believe us. I say," he called through the half-open door to the girls; "talk about adventures and things happening. We ought to be able to get some fun out of a magic carpet *and* a Phoenix."

"Rather," said the girls, in bed.

"Children," said father, on the stairs, "go to sleep at once. What do you mean by talking at this time of night?"

No answer was expected to this question, but under the bedclothes Cyril murmured one.

204

"Mean?" he said. "Don't know what we mean. I don't know what *anything* means—"

"But we've got a magic carpet *and* a Phoenix," said Robert.

"You'll get something else if father comes in and catches you," said Cyril. "Shut up, I tell you."

Robert shut up. But he knew as well as you do that the adventures of that carpet and that Phoenix were only just beginning. . . .

FOR FURTHER READING

Ashton, John. *Curious Creatures in Zoology*. London: John C. Nimms, 1890.

Borges, Jorge Luis. *The Book of Imaginary Beings*. New York: E. P. Dutton, 1969.

Browne, Sir Thomas. *Pseudodoxia Epidemica (Enquiries into Vulgar and Common Errors)*. London, 1646.

Burton, Richard F., trans. *The Arabian Nights* (also known as *The Book of the Thousand Nights and a Night*).

Clair, Colin. *Unnatural History*. New York: Abelard-Schuman, 1967.

Gesner, Conrad. *Historia animalium* (vols. I–V). Original Latin edition: Zurich, 1551–87.

Herodotus. *The Histories,* trans. by George Rawlinson. London, 1858. Various modern editions.

Krutch, Joseph Wood. *The World of Animals*. New York: Simon & Schuster, 1961.

Ley, Willy. *Willy Ley's Exotic Zoology*. New York: The Viking Press, 1959.

Lum, Peter. *Fabulous Beasts*. New York: Pantheon Books, 1951.

Magnus, Archbishop Olaus. *History of the Northern People,* 1555.

Pliny. *The Natural History of Pliny,* trans. by John Bostock and H. T. Riley. London: Henry G. Bohn, 1855.

Polo, Marco. *The Book of Marco Polo,* trans. by Sir Henry Yule. London: John Murray, 1875.

Pontoppidan, Bishop Erich. *The Natural History of Norway*. London, 1755.

Purchas, Samuel. *Purchas His Pilgrimes*. London, 1625. Modern edition, Glasgow: James MacLehose & Sons, 1905.

Silverberg, Robert. *The World of the Ocean Depths*. New York: Meredith Press, 1968.

Topsell, Edward. *History of Four-Footed Beasts*. London, 1658. Facsimile reprint, New York: Da Capo Press, 1967.